Numpty!

– A Guide to Lovable Thickoes

First published in Great Britain in 2011

Prion Books
an imprint of the
Carlton Publishing Group
20 Mortimer Street
London W1T 3JW

A catalogue record for this book is available from the British Library

ISBN 978-1-85375-819-5

Printed and bound by CPI Group (UK) Ltd, Croydon, CR0 4YY

10 9 8 7 6 5 4 3 2 1

Numpty!

– A Guide to Lovable Thickoes

Mike Haskins

Contents

1

What is a Numpty?

So just what is a Numpty?

In case you haven't noticed, it's not hard to find numpties nowadays. The world is suddenly full of them.

This is of course because older measures of idiocy such as the 'twerp', the 'buffoon' and the 'silly sod' have recently been phased out and replaced with the new international standard of idiocy, the 'numpty'.

This guide has been compiled to tell you all you need to know about numpties and what sorts of annoyance, stress and physical injury they are likely to inflict upon you.

But what exactly is a Numpty?

- Numpties are mini-potential disaster areas who walk among us every day. They seem so dim and hopeless that we tolerate and perhaps even pity them.

- Numpties are the people who never fail to get it wrong.

- Numpties are the ones who can't be trusted to do the simplest job without buggering it up. Numpties are the ones who are not only all thumbs but also butter-fingered, not to mention cack-handed, at the same time.

- Numpties are the ones who always manage to get the wrong end of the stick or, alternatively, who hand the stick to you so you end up with the wrong end of the stick (and a particularly shitty stick it invariably turns out to be). And it's impossible to go anywhere without tripping over a numpty: possibly literally.

- You can't drive round the block without a numpty pulling out in front of you.

- You can't walk round your local supermarket without a numpty running you down with their trolley.

- You can't go to work without finding yourself surrounded by numpties.

- You can't switch on your TV without seeing a numpty doing something stupid or saying something stupid.

- You probably can't even turn over in bed without bumping straight into a numpty.

What is a Numpty?

- If you fall ill, it will be with something you caught off a contagious numpty who didn't have the sense to stay at home.

- If you get soaked it will be because the numpty who comes on after the news got the forecast wrong.

- If you quietly confide a secret to a numpty, they will repeat it back in a voice so loud it can be heard in the next town.

- If something breaks in your home, it will have been installed by a numpty workman or, alternatively, by your numpty partner trying a spot of numpty DIY.

- If you lose your money it will be because you invested it in the Bradford and Numpty Building Society.

- And in case you had failed to notice, the essential requirement for political office in this country is to be a numpty.

- As far as the government is concerned, it doesn't matter who you vote for; the numpties always get in.

- If it weren't for numpties you would probably lead an uneventful, trouble-free life.

- And the worst thing of all is that these numpties will often be so dim that they think that you're the numpty, not them.

- But then, of course, they would think that.

- Well, after all, they are numpties.

Don't say 'Numpty'; say 'about as much use as…'

- A chocolate teapot.

- A waterproof teabag.

- An ashtray on a motorbike.

- A solar-powered torch.

- A Braille speedometer.

- An inflatable dartboard.

- A roll of non-stick Sellotape.

- A lead parachute.

- A concrete trampoline.

- A condom vending machine in the Vatican.

- A one-legged man at an arse-kicking contest.

- A sunroof in a submarine.

- A trap-door on a lifeboat.

- An ejector seat in a helicopter.

Ways to identify a Numpty in a large group

- Shout 'Oi, numpty!' And see who turns towards you with a hopeful smile on their face.

- Announce that everyone except the numpties has just won a prize, and watch to see who looks disappointed.

- Ask the crowd which of them has come along with a numpty and see who whispers to their partner not to say anything.

- Tell everyone there's a fire drill and they need to assemble in three rows: males, females, numpties.

- See who comes forward when you say there's a call for a numpty on the line while wandering round holding up a small toy phone.

- Announce that you're going to play a game of Pin the Tail On the Numpty and see who looks alarmed and attempts to cover their backside.

- Say 'Is it just me, or can anyone else smell a numpty?'; Then watch to see who has a crafty sniff of their armpits to check.

- Tell everyone the government has started issuing fines for being a numpty and see who looks worried.

Polite(-ish) names for Numpties

Calling someone a numpty is a quick, concise way of referring to an annoying but harmless idiot. Because it is so quick and concise, it helps save time. This is useful, because this time can then be used to clear up any mess or damage that the aforesaid numpty has just caused.

There are, of course, lots of other terms you can use when referring to a numpty.

Here are some of the politer ones:

- Buffoon, oaf, silly billy, silly sausage, silly bugger, silly beggar, Simple Simon, clown, twit, twerp, twonk, foolish fellow, bozo, birdbrain, lame-brain, scatterbrain, blockhead, bonehead, fathead, pinhead, dunderhead, softhead, buffoon, dimwit, nitwit, halfwit, dolt, dope, dork, dullard, fool, tomfool, foolish fellow, goof ball, idiot, ignoramus, imbecile, moron, nincompoop, ninny, numbskull, oaf, simpleton, clot, clod, clown, cretin, dunce, sap, pantaloon, laughing stock, lummox, dummy, dunce, jackass, turkey, twit, one of life's victims, ninny, mooncalf, chump, wally, duffer, booby, galoot, Charlie, dumbo, dimbo, dipstick, durbrain, gimboid, lemon, muppet, nana, pillock, plonker, pranny, prat, wazzock, muncer, willy worm.

The word is Numpty

Although its derivation is probably somewhat different, the word 'numpty' seems to combine the word 'numbskull' with the name of well-known disaster-prone egg-person 'Humpty Dumpty' (aka the green, inert, permanently grinning stuffed toy regularly featured on long-running children's TV series *Play School*).

'Numpty' thus seems a perfect way to describe an ineffectual, possibly ovoid, idiot who is wont to sit around in a hapless manner waiting until catastrophe strikes.

But where did this oh-so-useful expression come from?

The word 'numpty' is said to be derived from the obsolete Scottish expression 'numps'. This term, meaning a stupid person, possibly dates back to the 16th century.

The number of numpties living in Scotland must have burgeoned over the next 400 years because a survey in 2007 revealed that 'numpty' was the most popular expression then in use in Scotland.

The same year the term reached a world audience when actress Ashley Jensen used it during an episode of the US TV series *Ugly Betty*.

The first published use of 'numpty' is believed to have been in 1988 when the quotation 'How is it I get all the numpties in my class?' Was included in *The Patter: Another Blast*, a guide to Glasgow slang expressions by Michael Munro.

Scottish people, it seems, make frequent reference to numpties in their conversation. For example, those who have to spend much of their lives attempting to get numpties to understand what they are saying are wont to use the following popular Scottish expression: 'No. That wisnae wit I meant, ya big numpty!'

When it is the turn of a numpty to respond during conversation, they will inevitably come out with some complete nonsense. On such occasions Scots will tell them: 'Away an' bile yer heid, ya numpty; ye dinnae ken whit yer talkin' aboot!'

And those who have to spend much of their lives trying to sort out problems created by numpties frequently express their frustration by using the much loved Scottish saying: 'Ah, Jeez! Which numpty did this?'

Yes; the existence of so many numpties in the world is clearly threatening to turn all of us Scottish.

But why would the Scots have come up with such a term in the first place? What possible use would the nation that gave us Gillian McKeith, the Scottish football team and men in kilts, sporrans and tartan bobble-hats have for a word like 'numpty'?

Could it be that Scotland is in fact the home of some of the world's most notable numpties?

What is a Numpty?

Back in 2008 the word 'numpty' was given a further boost in popularity when, during an interview on BBC Radio 5 Live, author Frederick Forsyth referred to the Prime Minister of Great Britain as a 'numpty'.

Scottish person Gordon Brown had become PM in 2007. By an extraordinary coincidence, this was exactly one year before 'numpty' was voted the most popular word in Scotland.

And so with someone with the shape, personality and good fortune of an egg at Number 10, numpties seemed poised to take over the world...

Places You Are Likely To Find A Numpty

- Standing right in your way when you are trying to see something, get something or go somewhere.

- Anywhere and everywhere you go no matter how hard you try to avoid them.

- Locked in a lavatory.

- Stuck in a lift which they have recently broken.

- Stuck in a revolving door.

- At the bottom of a large hole into which they have recently fallen.

- Standing in some dog poo.

- Standing on your toe.

- Standing on their own being avoided by everyone.

- Standing on an area of sand that has recently become cut off by the tide.

- Talking to someone who desperately wants to get away.

- At some distance from wherever they are meant to be.

The Numpty brain

- He has two brains; one is lost, the other is out looking for it.

- He has one brain cell, and it is fighting for dominance.

- He hasn't got enough brains to give himself a headache.

- He is the world's only living brain donor.

- He was standing in the wrong queue when they were giving out the brains.

- He has discovered that the way to compensate for a tiny brain is to pretend to be dead.

- His mouth is in gear but his brain is in neutral.

- He is considering suing his brain for non-support.

- If brains were taxed, he would be entitled to a rebate.

- Someone cancelled the direct debit for his brain.

- If brains were bird droppings, he'd have a clean cage.

- If brains were dynamite he'd have nothing to worry about.

- If brains were dynamite, he wouldn't have enough to blow his nose.

- If he had brains, he'd take them out and play with them.

- He donated his brain to science before he had finished using it.

- He donated his brain to science but science sent it back.

- He donated his brain to science but science thought it was a new strain of bacteria.

- He has a Teflon brain. Nothing sticks to it.

- He has a very powerful brain. No thoughts can penetrate it.

- He had water on the brain, so it shrank.

- When he shakes his head you can hear his brain rattle like a pebble in a tin bucket.

- He has a brand-new brain. It's never been used.

- He has a perfectly good brain. He just has to work out how to install it.

Numpty spotting

We are frequently told that you should never go by first impressions. Well, that's all very well, but numpties can usually be identified as such in extraordinarily quick time, and from quite a long distance away. This is often because they are dressed in loud or ridiculously un-stylish clothes that only a numpty would choose to wear (possibly smeared with the remains of a recent meal).

Other ways in which numpties can be spotted from a long distance include:

- the fact that they may have just caused some sort of injury to themselves or others;

- that they may have just set off some sort of alarm;

- that emergency vehicles will be gathered around them;

- that they may just have caused a nearby building to be evacuated by accidentally setting fire to it;

- that they may just have accidentally set fire to themselves;

- or that they may have just been responsible for some minor disaster or foolish misunderstanding that has caused their cheeks to glow with embarrassment and the group around them to start chanting at them as one: 'You numpty!'

Even without such obvious visual clues as the presence of the emergency services, smouldering ruins and chanting crowds, it is usually very easy to identify a numpty.

Often by the time a numpty has finished saying 'Hello' to you, you will be fully aware of their numptiness.

Generally speaking, a numpty will introduce him/herself to you by apologizing.

If they don't, they will introduce themselves by doing something for which they should apologize.

Sometimes a numpty may have no choice but to introduce him/herself to you because he/she has just caused you, your car, your property or an elderly member of your family some significant damage. In such cases the numpty will probably introduce themselves to you by saying 'Hello', followed by 'I'm sorry', followed by 'Here are my insurance details.'

Health and safety laws should surely be introduced forcing numpties to be adapted to make a warning beeping sound whenever they approach. Alternatively numpties should be preceded by a man with a red flag walking in front of them at all times.

Ways in which a Numpty will introduce him/herself to you for the very first time

- By spilling a drink over you.

- By stepping forward to greet you and treading on your toe in the process.

- By accidentally spitting something they have recently been eating into your eye while attempting to say 'Hello'.

- By standing up to greet you and in the process tipping the contents of a small table over you.

- By extending a hand to greet you and in the process accidentally slapping a small child in the face.

- By enthusiastically embracing you before realizing a moment later that you are not the person that they thought you were.

- By embracing you in such a way that items you are each wearing become inextricably bound together.

- By embracing you, losing their balance and dragging you to the ground with them in the process.

- By falling down a flight of stairs on top of you and using you to break their fall.

How to spot a Numpty at a party

- They turn up apparently having made a unilateral decision that your party is a fancy dress party.

- They arrive earlier than anyone else: possibly several days earlier.

- They brought a bottle, but dropped it on the way.

- In a determined effort to get the party started they begin madly dancing and gyrating in the front room (even though there isn't any music playing yet).

- In a determined effort to get the party started they begin madly dancing and gyrating in the front room before realizing they are in the wrong house.

- They vomit into a pot plant on the mantelpiece, sometimes before they have had anything to drink.

- They attempt to get off with either:
    a. someone whose partner is standing right next to them,
    b. someone's parent who is dropping them off, or
    c. a neighbour who has come round to complain about the noise.

- They presume the member of the police force called out following complaints from the neighbours is a stripper and start trying to remove their uniform.

Enter the Numpty: advice for Numpties on the simple act of entering buildings

Glass doors

These are always good to walk straight into. Go ahead and knock yourself out: quite literally. For added hilarity, try doing this while carrying a hot drink or tray of food items.

Locked out

Most people check they have their keys before closing the door behind them. Numpties check afterwards.

Keys left in the door

Numpties will spend hours looking all over the house for their keys, only to find they left them dangling in the lock when they came in. The keys could thus be picked up by a passing burglar who would then be able to let himself into the house at his leisure and lock up again after completing his burglary business.

Leaving something just behind a door

A popular numpty booby-trap. Leave a small object right behind a door. Then when the next person pushes the door, it will open for a second before rebounding on their surprised face just as they are stepping through.

Getting their clothes stuck in the door

Numpties move so quickly that their scarves and ties constantly swirl out behind them. These can then become caught in closing doors, so bringing the numpty to an abrupt halt. The numpty may then also find that the door is locked and cannot be reopened.

Slamming the door

Angry or careless numpties often slam the door behind them. They then have to come back in to find out which object just fell off a shelf and shattered as a result of their door-slamming.

Leaving the door open to slam on its own

Numpties may forget to close the door at all, leaving a gust of wind to slam it shut. The resulting unexpected noise will cause panic that an intruder is in the house, something else to fall off a shelf and smash on the floor and someone of a nervous disposition to have a heart attack.

Pulling when it says 'Push'

Or pushing when it says 'Pull'. Whatever it says on the door, numpties do the opposite.

Aspects of their appearance that Numpties will only notice when they get back home

Numpties! Award yourself ten bonus numpty points for every one of the following. See how many you can achieve simultaneously.

Bogey hanging out of nose

All day long the numpty has been out and about at work, meeting friends and attending important meetings. Unfortunately, all this time there has been a small green object hanging out of one of the numpty's nostrils playing a game of peek-a-boo with every person he has met. Oh, well. No wonder everyone was staring wide eyed into his face. He thought it was because they couldn't believe how good-looking he was.

Big yellow spot on nose

This is another good way for a numpty to hold the attention of those with whom he chooses to share his wisdom during the day. They may even make themselves go cross-eyed in their attempts to focus their eyes on the golden excrescence rising from the numpty's bulbous red nose.

Bit on the teeth

What could be more unpleasant than most of an entire spinach leaf being left plastered across a numpty's front teeth following a delicious lunch? This lump of green matter will then intermittently flash into view every time the numpty gives someone one of his great beaming numpty smiles.

Toothpaste round the mouth

At least this shows that the numpty gives his teeth a good brush in the morning. Unfortunately the numpty has come away from the morning ablutions with an area of white toothpaste still daubed round his mouth that makes him look a bit like Coco the Clown.

The numpty will then add to this effect by continually sticking his great pink tongue out in front of everyone and revolving it round the edges of his mouth trying without success to lick away the fresh, minty-tasting toothpaste.

Not properly dressed

Numpties have trouble dressing themselves. Shirt buttons may be threaded through incorrect holes, non-matching pairs of shoes or socks may be worn and jumpers put on back to front.

What is a Numpty?

Massive black hair sprouting from the depths of one nostril

A numpty will often sport one or more magnificent hairs dangling from their nostrils like exotic plants. The effect is even better if combined with a bogey hanging out of the nose. A numpty can then create an effect not unlike having a little green Quasimodo figure bouncing up and down out of their nose as though on the end of a miniature bell-rope.

Flies wide open

The ever-popular trouser style favoured by male numpties. The numpty will, of course, have made some attempt to do up his zip, but the zip will then decide to surreptitiously descend while he's not looking, so revealing the numpty's underpants (or worse) for all to see. The more open the trousers, the longer the numpty will take to realize why everyone he meets does nothing but look down in horror at his crotch. For a while the numpty will presume that this look of horror is in fact one of awe and admiration at his taste in corduroy pants.

Hair blown into bizarre style

The slightest breeze is capable of re-sculpting a numpty's hairdo. Following a tiny gust of wind, 90 per cent of a numpty's hair will suddenly be on one side of their head pointing directly upwards. Somehow the hair will then remain in this random styling for the rest of the day.

Shaving cuts

Male numpties' faces and female numpties' legs will regularly appear to resemble something from a slasher horror film. A male numpty will regularly shave his stubbly beard off and replace it with a beard of tiny red scabs which the numpty can then knock open every time he strokes his chin, thereby unleashing yet more gore upon a horrified world.

Wardrobe malfunction

Numpties are so inept at dressing themselves that various bits of their bodies will appear peeking out of gaps in their clothes. Numpty nipples, buttocks, testicles etc., can thus be seen peeping out at passers-by while their numpty owner remains somehow unaware of the situation, despite the discomfort and the chilly sensation that must surely be involved.

Bird poo on head

Inadvertently finding yourself covered in bird droppings is a problem usually only encountered by newly-cleaned cars and the sandpaper at the bottom of a budgie's cage. If, however, you place a numpty in an open space, he too will seem to attract bird plop towards himself. Even if there seem to be no birds in the vicinity, poop will nevertheless home in on a numpty. The principal is akin to that of lightning seeking the shortest route between the cloud and the ground below by using any high object that stands out in a landscape. Avian excreta will similarly choose the numptiest route between a bird's bottom and the ground below. Thus adorned, a numpty will spend the day wandering around with peculiar grey highlights in his hair or small, oddly-shaped epaulettes balanced on his shoulders. If the numpty has been targeted by a particularly large bird, he may wonder why he suddenly finds himself wearing a hat that he cannot remember putting on.

Damp patch on the crotch

A circular area on the front of a man's trousers that is several shades darker than the surrounding material is a horrifying sight that clearly identifies the wearer to be a numpty. This is the telltale sign that a male numpty was in a bit too much of a hurry to get back from the toilet. The numpty's attitude was clearly to not bother perfecting his shaking technique. Instead, the numpty just popped his little fellow back in his pants as soon as it seemed to have stopped going. Then, when the numpty had left the urinal and taken about three steps out of the toilet door, the little numpty in his pants suddenly and unexpectedly decided to do a short encore, perhaps lasting several seconds. Possibly the numpty wondered about trying to dash back to the lavatory, or maybe he thought nobody would notice that he was now walking round with a vertical puddle on his trousers that clearly demonstrated to all spectators which side he dressed.

Bit of shirt sticking out of trouser fly

For an even greater touch of class than the traditional wide-open, trouser fly why not position a little bit of shirt tail sticking out of the gaping zip? The exposed bit of shirt will then appear to others to be a small imitation penis. Passers-by will be so distracted by this effect that traffic accidents may occur as a result.

Skirt tucked into pants

Female numpties were clearly unhappy with all the attention that male numpties were able to attract by wandering around with their flies open, and so they invented the idea of accidentally hitching the hem of their skirt up and tucking it into the back of their underwear before leaving the lavatory. The female numpty can then walk around for the rest of the day in this exhibitionist state without a single person being brave enough to tell them. And for an even greater touch of class on this option, why not try adopting the same style while wearing a thong?

Food round the mouth

Squirrels store surplus food inside their cheeks. Numpties do something similar, but using the outside of their cheeks. After finishing eating, a numpty usually has about 50 per cent of his meal still spread over his face. Unfortunately numpties seem completely unaware when they leave the dinner table with a face resembling a plate ready for the dishwasher. This is because the edges of numpty mouths are the second least sensitive part of their bodies (after their brains). A numpty therefore spends the hours following each meal with enough material spread over his face to fill a sandwich. Anyone who has to gaze upon the numpty's face for any length of time will be horrified by the sight. They will then start sticking their own tongue out and licking away at their own mouth as though the food mess is on their face rather than that of the numpty. Not only will this action fail to remove the tasty material, but the numpty may mistake it for some kind of sexual come-on.

Did you hear about the Numpty...

- ...who heard that most car accidents happen within two miles of home, so he moved?

- ...who made the mistake of reversing into a car boot sale, but on the plus side managed to sell his engine for a fiver?

- ...who tried to kill himself by taking an overdose of aspirin, but after he'd had a couple started to feel a lot better?

- ...who tried hitch-hiking but decided to get up early to try and avoid the traffic?

- ...who tried to swim the Channel but halfway across realized he wasn't going to make it, so swam back?

- ...who tried to get away with just a photocopy of his old TV licence because all he ever watched was repeats?

- ...who got back to his office after lunch and saw a sign saying 'Back in 30 minutes', so he sat down to wait for himself?

- ...who lit a match to see if he'd blown out the candle?

- ...who sold his car to get money for petrol?

Things a Numpty couldn't do...

- He couldn't organize a piss-up in a brewery.

- He couldn't organize a fart in a chilli-eating contest.

- He couldn't pull the skin off a custard.

- He couldn't run a bath.

- He couldn't think his way out of a paper bag.

- He couldn't empty water out of a bucket with the instructions printed on the bottom.

- He couldn't find a football in a wash tub.

- He couldn't find his arse with both hands and a map.

- He couldn't hit sand if he fell off a camel.

- He couldn't hit the floor if he fell on it.

- He couldn't pick the winner of a one-horse race.

- He couldn't see through a ladder.

- He couldn't spell 'cat' if you helped him with the first two letters.

Clothes only Numpties will wear

Bow tie

An item of clothing that makes it look as though a terrifyingly huge breed of moth is nesting just below your neck. Suitable wear for numpties only.

Braces

Big, colourful elastic strips to hold your trousers up. When wearing them you will be unable to resist pulling them out and then releasing them suddenly. This will cause your trouser bottoms to be pulled up at the same time and the elastic to then snap back into your chest. Braces are therefore large, catapult-like devices designed to help you attack your own nipples: clearly intended for numpties.

Brightly coloured waistcoats

A waistcoat would be bad enough. Waistcoats with luminous embroidered patterns or images will only be worn by the sort of person who wants other people to know that they are a numpty even if the other person is standing some distance away.

Flared trousers

Designed to make a numpty's ankles look twice as fat as their thighs.

Shoulder pads

Popular in the 1980s and designed to make female numpties look as though they had thrown a jacket on and in the process covered up two small parrots that they had balanced on either shoulder.

G-string

A long-running April Fool joke that involved someone telling a female numpty that a pirate's eye patch from a fancy dress outfit was in fact an item of sexy underwear. Not only is this very uncomfortable, but it immediately disappears up your bottom and then advertises the fact it has disappeared up your bottom to everyone around you every time you slightly bend over.

Corset

It might make you look thinner, but it also stops you breathing and brings your digestive process to a standstill. As soon as it is loosened you will be unable to prevent yourself breaking wind continuously for the next quarter of an hour.

Low-rise jeans

Specially designed to make anyone appear incapable of pulling their pants up.

Torn jeans

A way to sell damaged goods to numpties for large amounts of money.

2

Numpties
at Work

Numptiness in the office workplace

You might think it surprising that any numpty could manage to get a job: but look around. Who can honestly say they don't have one or two numpties among their work colleagues? In fact, is it one or two, or is it wall-to-wall numpties where you work? And don't forget all the bosses you've had during your career. Wasn't being a numpty high on the list of requirements when they applied for their jobs?

Yes; when you think about it, your own workplace is pretty much a numpty-only zone. So what's going on? Is there some sort of equal opportunity programme in place forcing employers to hire numpties? Or is it just the fact that so many organizations are already almost entirely staffed by numpties that they like to fill any vacancies with those like themselves? It's probably best not to think what that says about you.

But what are some of the favourite bits of numptiness that your numpty colleagues will get up to in the office?

Coming into work with a horrible contagious illness

Many sensible employees (such as yourself) phone in sick if they wake up with so much as a slight sniffle. After all, this is merely consideration for your fellow workers. You don't want your colleagues to fall ill and suffer the discomfort of a slight runny nose as well, do you?

Numpties, however, have no such concerns and will bravely soldier into work while suffering from everything from a nasty cold through to bubonic plague, botulism and bird flu. They will then sit in the middle of the office coughing and sneezing in your general direction until your life expectancy has been reduced by several years. Numpties will often do this a day or two before you are due to enjoy a much-anticipated holiday, which you will now spend in your hotel room feeling like death.

This display of inconsiderate numptiness is also irritating because it raises your boss's expectations of how ill anyone in your office should be before they take a day off sick.

Forwarding your rude email to everyone

A classic numpty manoeuvre. You make the mistake of sending an email to a numpty workmate during the course of which you make a rude comment about one of your other colleagues (eg., the boss). Your numpty pal then finds this so hilarious they decide to share your email with everyone they know – starting with the colleague (eg., the boss) about whom you made the rude comment.

And if your numpty chum doesn't do this on purpose, they will achieve the same ends by accident. When they reply to you, they will accidentally press a button on their computer that no one has ever previously noticed and which automatically forwards your email. A moment later everyone in the known world will be reading your amusing comments about your boss's bad breath or noticeable bottom hair. You might as well start clearing your desk straight away: or maybe go and declaim your rude comment very loudly straight into your boss's face. You might as well get some pleasure out of the situation.

Forgetting to pass on a phone message

Your most important client phones. You are not at your desk. The most helpful, cheerful person in the office steps forward to answer your phone. Unfortunately the most helpful, cheerful person in the office will inevitably be a numpty. A message of extreme importance will be taken. Your client will be assured by the numpty that you will return his call or deal with the matter in question immediately. The numpty will then forget to pass on the important phone message.

The first you will ever hear of it will be several days later when you are called into your boss's office to be told, in no particular order, that you are losing your job, that your most important client is furious that you didn't return his call and that he is withdrawing his company's business with immediate effect.

A few days after this, during your farewell drink in the pub, the numpty will sidle up to you and say, 'I forgot to tell you; one of your clients phoned the other day…'

Breaking the photocopier

Numpties in offices are for ever being given the photocopying to do. This is considered a reasonably safe job for them to perform. It isn't.

The first problem is the length of time the numpty will spend at the photocopier. If you are next in line to use the machine, you can find yourself waiting there for much of the day while the numpty photocopies their way through what appears to be the complete published works of the human race.

This situation will not, of course, last for ever: but this is not a good thing. Eventually the numpty will quietly collect their eight-foot-high stack of photocopied sheets from the machine and stagger back to their desk. Unfortunately this does not mean that you will now be able to start doing your copying. There is only one reason why a numpty ever stops photocopying, and that is because they have just broken the photocopier. If photocopiers didn't break down, numpties would stand next to them cheerfully copying away until the sun collapses.

As soon as they have successfully knackered the office photocopier, the numpty will decide to slip quietly away and allow the next person in line (ie., you) to sort the problem out. When you step forward you will be greeted by an array of flashing lights and warning symbols on the operating panel. These will make the machine look less like a photocopier than a pinball machine. Forty minutes later you will have your sleeves rolled up and be lying under the machine like an engineer with your clothes and hands covered in mysterious photocopying chemicals while you take the entire thing to pieces.

And then as soon as you get it all working again and go back to your desk for something, the numpty will re-appear at the photocopier to continue his/her life's work of buggering it all up again. And so hence the traditional joke:

Q: What do you call the person who's next in line behind a numpty to use the photocopier?

A: The photocopier repair man.

Emptying the stationery cupboard

If you wonder why you can never find a pen, stapler or envelope in the stationery cupboard no matter how often you go there, try checking the top drawer of a numpty's desk. There you will find an extraordinary horde of material which the numpty keeps taking from the stationery cupboard.

The numpty's logic is impeccable; it is necessary to stockpile this material because the stationery cupboard itself always seems to be empty. I wonder why that is.

Putting their used pens back in the stationery cupboard

One item you will find in abundance in the office stationery cupboard is old biros with one end, or possibly both, well chewed by numpty teeth. For some reason numpties think it will be helpful if they put their old pens back in the stationery cupboard once they have run out. You can then spend another happy few hours going backwards and forwards from your desk trying to find a pen that still contains sufficient ink to write more than one sentence.

Breaking the lift

Among the many mechanical disasters that numpties like to inflict on the workplace, breaking the lift is a pièce de résistance.

If you ever step into a lift and you hear a numpty cheerfully ask, 'Which floor?' You know you're in trouble. The numpty will be standing with a finger poised ready to jab at the lift's controls. As far as you're concerned, it's the finger of doom. The lift controls will be relatively simple, perhaps only comprising two or three buttons. Numpties will, however, have perfected the art of pressing the buttons in such a way that the lift will cease to function.

This will not happen immediately, of course. Having been designed and installed by numpties, the lift will instead travel a few feet, so it is between floors. It will then cease to function and you will be left in a small, confined space for several hours with a numpty for company.

Numpties usually like to perform this trick at going-home time on Friday afternoon.

Finding hitherto unknown buttons on your computer

If a numpty ever asks if they can borrow your computer for just a second, say no. No matter how many years you have been using the machine, no matter how familiar you are with your office systems, a numpty will accidentally press a button that you have never previously noticed. A message will then start flashing on screen that all your files are being deleted. The numpty will tell you not to worry because he knows how to fix this. After he has attempted to fix it, the message will change to read that your files are being deleted permanently.

Getting promoted

Laws exist that prevent employers from sacking people simply on the basis that they are numpties. Only one way therefore remains to get a numpty out of a job where they are proving to be disastrous, and this is to promote them.

Numpties thus ascend the scale of management to form what is known as the 'numpty layer', which can be found in almost all organizations.

Numpty responses to job interview questions

Q: Where do you see yourself in five years?

A: In your chair, handing you your redundancy papers, granddad!

Q: What did you do in your previous job?

A: As little as possible.

Q: What do you think are the advantages of working here?

A: Free stationery and all the hours on Facebook I need.

Q: Did you think of applying to any our competitors?

A: Yes. None of them would have me.

Q: What do you think you'll bring to this job?

A: Some sandwiches, an apple and a flask.

Q: What sort of experience have you had using computers?

A: Do porn sites count?

Q: What led you to apply here?

A: A threat from the benefit office.

Q: Your CV shows excellent experience for this job, but what would you say are your main strengths?

A: I'm an extremely convincing liar.

Q: Why did you leave your last job?

A: It turned out that Dress Down Friday didn't stretch as far as naturism.

Q: What would you say are your weaknesses?

A: Redheads, Battenberg and kryptonite.

Q: Describe how you would deal with an awkward customer.

A: Erotic massage.

Q: What are your interests outside work?

A: Drug and alcohol abuse, stalking, international terrorism, voodoo and morris dancing.

Q: How would you describe yourself in one word?

A: Satan.

Q: And finally, have you got any questions for us?

A: Yes; what is it you do here again?

A: Will you be checking which websites I visit?

A: Why didn't you ask about my prison record?

A: Do my exam certificates look genuine to you?

A: Precisely how much sick leave can I get away with each month?

A: Why do bad things happen to good people?

A: Did you just fart in the middle of my interview?

A: If I get the job, could you give me an idea of exactly how difficult it'll be for you to sack me?

Top-secret security passwords chosen by Numpties to protect their computers

- The word 'password'.

- Or, for extra security, the phrase 'secretpassword'.

- Or, to really fool the hackers, 'password1'.

- Or the cunning numerical sequence '123456789'.

- Or, even more cunningly, '987654321'.

- Or their name (eg., 'mrnumpty').

- Or, if they're even numptier than that, 'me' (which they think of as their name).

- Or the name of their pet (eg., 'dog').

- Or 'donaldduckmickeymousetomandjerrybugsbunny' (when told their password must be at least five characters).

- Or 'atleast5characters' (when told their password must be at least 5 characters).

- Or '****', because that always seems to come up on screen no matter what they type.

Great moments in Numpty history

The computer

2400 BC	Invention of the abacus.
2399 BC	A Numpty somehow manages to crash his abacus and then slip over on the beads as they spill over the floor.
1822	Charles Babbage designs the Difference Engine, the world's first mechanical computer.
1823	A numpty designs the world's first Difference Engine virus.
7th Aug 1944	IBM's Automatic Sequence Controlled Calculator was given to Harvard University. It weighed five tons and was 51 feet long.
8th Aug 1944	A numpty gives himself a hernia trying to get one up the stairs so he can install it in his back bedroom.
1950	Alan Turing develops the Turing Test, a test to ascertain whether a mechanical device is capable of responding to questions with human-like intelligence.
1951	A Numpty manages to fail the Turing Test.
1961	First email sent.
1962	A numpty invents spam.

Hairstyles favoured by Numpties

The comb-over

Much used by bald numpties, but it fools no one, and if there's the slightest breeze you will suddenly have a completely bald head and one very hairy shoulder.

Bit sticking out at the side

Worn by numpties who, after lying on one side in bed, get up to find that half of their hair is sticking out at right angles from their head.

The angled fringe

Sported by wrinklies who have attempted to cut their own hair and ended up with a fringe rising at a 45 degree angle across their forehead, thus making it look as though they are wearing a wig which has slipped slightly.

The pudding bowl

Someone is a real numpty if they not only have this Richard III-style haircut but flecks of treacle sponge and custard all over it.

The same haircut they had 30 years ago

Numpties like to maintain their hair in a style that serves as a sort of shrine to the era in which they grew up.

Numpties in photographs

Things numpties will be doing when caught in a group photo:

- Looking in a different direction to everyone else.

- Making bunny ears behind someone's head.

- Sticking their tongue out.

- Pouting in a faintly nauseating manner.

- Picking their nose.

- Adjusting their genitals.

- Gazing with intense interest at someone's breasts.

- Grinning madly when everyone else in the shot is looking solemn.

- Looking solemn when everyone else in the shot is grinning madly.

- Wrinkling their nose in disgust as though the person next to them has passed wind.

- Appearing on the verge of losing their balance.

Photographs taken by Numpties

Telltale signs that a photograph was taken by a numpty:

- It's out of focus.

- The heads of the people being photographed don't feature in the shot.

- The heads of the people being photographed just about creep into the very bottom of the shot.

- A dark shadow completely envelops the scene.

- Everyone in the shot looks dazzled and has bright red spots where their eyes should be.

- The photo is largely blank apart from a tiny dot that was supposed to have been the subject of the picture.

- The photo is framed at a peculiar angle as though the photographer was falling over as it was taken.

- The person being photographed appears to have a large plant growing out of the top of their head.

- The photo has a large numpty finger intruding into it.

- It depicts the inside of the numpty's pocket or bag.

If brains were...

- If brains were lard, he'd be hard pressed to grease a small pan.

- If brains were lead weights, his would blow away.

- If brains were wood, his pet termite would starve.

- If brains were wood, he wouldn't have enough to make one small matchstick.

- If brains were deodorant, you'd smell him coming a mile off.

- If brains were flammable, he wouldn't require a smoke detector.

- If brains were money, he'd be filing for bankruptcy.

3

Numpty Drivers

Numpty drivers

You don't expect numpties to be good at exams. There is, however, one examination that numpties seem to have no trouble passing: the driving test. This is possibly because driving examiners are handing out passes to numpties in order to avoid the risk of having to go through another test with them a few weeks later. Alternatively, it's because driving lessons are in fact a process designed to teach numpties how to pretend they aren't numpties for just long enough to get through their driving tests. This explains both why the roads are full of numpties and why driving lessons are so expensive.

Once a numpty has posed as a non-numpty for the duration of their driving test, their true numpty nature will quickly return. Now not only are they a numpty; they are a numpty travelling at speed in a large metal object with bits that open and lights that flash. Suddenly they are no longer abiding by the Highway Code but by a system of driving known only to numpties.

Numpty drivers' favourite manoeuvres

Mirror, signal, manoeuvre

Numpties will follow this official procedure whenever pulling out in their numpty cars. Unfortunately they will very rarely follow the procedure in the correct order. Most often they will begin with 'manoeuvre', follow it with a 'signal' and then a look in the mirror to see what the crash was that just happened behind them. Indeed, sometimes numpties will simply 'manoeuvre'.

Emergency stop

Numpties are very good at doing this. They have to be. Usually they will practice this form of stopping every time they come to a halt for any reason whatsoever.

33-point turn

The numpty equivalent of the three-point turn. See also the 33.3333 recurring-point turn, which is the same thing but carrying on without end.

Reversing

This happens without warning when a numpty is driving due to their continuing uncertainty about how to work the gear lever.

Parallel parking

A method of parking used by numpties which involves smashing into at least two other vehicles.

Things that Numpty drivers often get mixed up

- The footbrake and the accelerator pedal.

- The handbrake and the gear stick.

- Forward and reverse.

- The indicator and windscreen wiper controls.

- The screen-wash button and the car horn.

- Which lane to be in.

- Which side of the road to drive on.

- Which window to look out of.

- Which way to turn the wheel when reversing.

- Which way to turn the wheel when going forward.

- Red and green traffic lights.

- Miles per hour and kilometres per hour.

- The width of their car and the narrowness of the gap.

- Unleaded and diesel.

Skills used by Numpties when driving

Telepathy

When changing lanes or moving off, numpty drivers will rely on the power of telepathy to communicate their intentions to fellow-road users rather than the more usual indicators. Numpties' psychic abilities are attested to by the fact that other drivers frequently comment, 'I knew that numpty was going to do that.'

The element of surprise

Another weapon in the numpty driver's arsenal. Numpty drivers will pull out when least expected, cut in when least wanted, turn in the opposite direction to that suggested by their indicators and suddenly stop when there doesn't seem to be anything to stop for (apart from to admire an interestingly shaped cloud formation passing overhead).

Perseverance

A skill used by numpties who have got a bit lost. Numpties believe that if they persevere for long enough, the road they are travelling along will eventually join up with the one they should be on. Numpties will not desist from this belief even as the unlikelihood of it happening becomes increasingly evident.

Indestructibility

Confidence in their own Captain Scarlet-like indestructibility inspires numpties to drive the way they do (ie., like a maniac who is late for an important meeting of his local maniacs' and speed freaks' association and who appears unaware of stopping distances, the Highway Code or the existence of other drivers).

Not asking for directions

Numpties usually refuse to ask for directions no matter how lost they are. If they do stop for directions they will immediately get bored and fail to listen to them.

Hand gestures

Numpty drivers like to communicate to other motorists by using hand gestures. They will sail past either waving, signalling or making obscene gestures at their fellow-drivers. They will do this to such an extent that they resemble the person signing for the deaf in the corner of TV programmes broadcast in the early hours of the morning.

Numpties may even take both hands off the steering wheel while driving in order to convey messages to other motorists through the power of mime.

Obeying everything the satnav says

Numpties tend to be rather sheep-like and will do whatever anyone tells them. Never is this demonstrated better than when a numpty continues to follow instructions from their satnav even though they have been driving up a canal for the past 20 minutes.

Vibration

Numpty drivers will drive with one wheel permanently on the rumble strip at the side of the road. This way they can keep driving in a straight line even if they nod off to sleep for a few moments.

Flashing headlights

Numpties will attempt to communicate with other drivers by flashing their headlights as though using a pair of portable Aldis lamps. It is unclear exactly what numpties are attempting to communicate by this process. Sometimes they may be saying 'You go first', or alternatively 'I'll go first' (leading to disastrous consequences if the other driver interprets the flashing incorrectly). Sometimes the flashing may mean 'Thank you', or 'Watch out', or 'Your car appears to be on fire', or 'This'll dazzle you, you bastard.'

Non-stop indicator

Numpties will frequently drive down the road blissfully unaware that one of their indicators is flashing away, suggesting to other drivers that they could make a turn at any point.

Convoy

Numpties will drive at needlessly slow speeds when travelling along roads where no overtaking is possible. This helps build up a long convoy of other vehicles behind the numpty car. Numpties like to do this because it is the only time others are forced to follow them. It thus gives them an unusual sense of popularity and leadership.

Parking

Even when numpties are not inside their cars, they will leave the vehicle in a position designed to ensure maximum numptiness and inconvenience to other road users. Numpties will leave their cars parked on pavements, in no-parking areas, across people's driveways, in the middle of the road, on roundabouts, blocking the entrance to a hospital, wedged up against other vehicles so their owners cannot get in except through the sunroof and just about anywhere that other drivers would never dream of parking.

Numpty answers in the practical driving test

Q: How you would check that your direction indicators are working correctly?

A: Make a turn and then check to see if the driver in the car behind is mouthing curses.

Q: How would you check your horn is working?

A: Drive up behind an elderly person, sound the horn and see how far they jump.

Q: How would you test your brakes?

A: If the elderly person turns out to be deaf.

Q: Show me where the reservoir is for your windscreen washer.

A: OK, but it's going to be a bit of a drive. I think it's in a valley in North Wales.

Q: Where is the dipstick?

A: Sitting right here next to you in the driver's seat.

Q: Open the bonnet, identify where the brake fluid reservoir is and tell me how you would check that you have a safe level of hydraulic brake fluid.

A: Which is the bonnet again?

Q: How would you check you have sufficient tread on your tyres?

A: Drive over someone and check what prints are left on their clothes.

Q: How would you check your oil level?

A: Get my doctor to give me a cholesterol test.

Q: How would you check your handbrake for wear?

A: Park on a hill and see if the car's still there when I've finished shopping.

Q: Can you read the registration plate of the heavy goods vehicle parked 20 metres away?

A: What heavy goods vehicle?

Q: How would you adjust the head restraint on your seat to provide the best protection in the event of a crash?

A: Put it in front of my face.

Q: How would you ensure you pass an emissions test?

A: Avoid eating beans.

Q: How do you know if your headlights are dipped?

A: Passers-by stop shielding their eyes.

Q: How would you check your rear lights?

A: Get my passenger to do the steering while I crawl back through the sunroof to have a look.

The Numpty approach to safe driving

Safe driving tip	The numpty approach
Check and adjust all mirrors before moving off.	Check yourself in the mirror and restyle your hair every time you stop at a junction.
Do not eat while driving.	A small cooking stove wedged between the front seats should be fine.
Do not drink and drive.	Wedge a minibar just behind the cooking stove.
Do not drive if feeling drowsy.	If you're not meant to drive while feeling drowsy, why does that big pillow keep coming out of the steering wheel every time you bump into anything?
Do not use your mobile phone while driving.	Why do they call it a mobile, then?
Make sure you know the meanings of all the warning indicators on your dashboard.	See if you can get all the pretty lights to come on at once.
Make sure you can see clearly through all windows.	Wipe a small, round area in the middle of the mist on the front windscreen and that should do.

Comments passengers are likely to make when in a car being driven by a Numpty

- Where are we?

- Do you think you should stop and ask someone for directions?

- Isn't that the same tree we went past an hour ago?

- Why are all the other cars on this road driving in the opposite direction to us?

- That ambulance/fire engine/police car is still right behind us trying to get past.

- Are you sure we can fit through that gap?

- I told you I didn't think we'd fit through that gap.

- The driver in the next car is making a gesture at us that isn't in the Highway Code.

- Can you see to drive through all the smoke coming from the bonnet?

- Are you sure this is a proper road?

- Is it best to open the window before or after we sink?

Great moments in Numpty history

The car

29th Jan 1886	Karl Benz patents the world's first car, the Benz Patent Motorwagen.
30th Jan 1886	A numpty purchases a Benz Patent Motorwagen.
30th Jan 1886	Karl Benz is slightly injured after being run over by one of his own Benz Patent Motorwagens as it was being driven out of the showroom.
31st Jan 1886	A numpty's neighbours are the first people in the world to be woken in the early hours by the sound of a car door being slammed.
31st Jan 1886	The numpty's neighbours get up to discover a Benz Patent Motorwagen parked across their driveway.
1st Feb 1886	A numpty gets the world's first parking ticket for his Benz Patent Motorwagen.
2nd Feb 1886	A numpty manages to lock his keys in his Benz Patent Motorwagen (which is quite an achievement, seeing as it was an open-topped vehicle).
3rd Feb 1886	A numpty crashes his Benz Patent Motorwagen.
4th Feb 1886	The world's first no-claims bonus is lost.

4

Shopping with Numpty

Shopping with Numpty

Another location where you are sure to run into numpties aplenty is when visiting the shops.

Numpties cannot resist shopping. Unfortunately an accumulation of numpties will build up during the course of the day in any shop, supermarket or shopping centre. This is because shops exist to take advantage of numpties. Why else is there so much rubbish for sale? Who would want to eat some of the inedible muck on offer at the supermarket? Who but a numpty would fall for dodgy special offers such as 'Two for the price of three' or 'Buy 1,860,753, get one free'? And so each day your local shops will fill up with numpties shuffling about like a plague of zombies mesmerized by the bright lights and colourful trinkets on display.

Visit your shops and you will find numpties everywhere: numpties trying to think what to buy, numpties getting in your way and numpties waiting to serve you at the cash till. But just what sort of annoyingly numptyish behaviour might you find at the supermarket?

Forgetting to buy the one thing they went for

Send a numpty to the shops to buy one essential item and half an hour later they will be back with a bag bulging with shopping – none of which you will really need. This is because the numpty spent the whole time they were in the shop walking up and down the aisles piling up stuff in their trolley in the vain hope that they would eventually remember the thing they were sent out for.

Failing to understand the special offers

Supermarkets must make a high percentage of their profits from numpties who fail to understand special offers. Numpties will stand for several minutes desperately trying to take in the offers advertised on supermarket shelves. They will then pick up a number of items that were not on their shopping list. These will, however, invariably fail to qualify for the advertised offer. The numpty will thus end up paying full price for a load of rubbish which they never wanted in the first place.

Standing in front of exactly the thing you want to buy

Numpties may have very small brains, but nevertheless they are equipped with extraordinary powers of telepathy. You can walk into a supermarket requiring only one single item. A numpty will, however, become mysteriously aware of your purpose and will make a bee-line for the very thing you want to buy. The numpty will stand right in front of you making an extraordinarily prolonged choice about which brand of jam to choose until you lose the will to live.

Going off to do more shopping while at the checkout

Despite having just wandered up and down every aisle of the supermarket, a numpty will get to the checkout having failed to remember half of the things on their shopping list. They will tell the till assistant they just need to get one more item and dash off past the half-mile-long queue of shoppers waiting behind them. Twenty minutes later they will return pushing another whole trolley piled high with stuff.

Picking up goods with no barcodes

Everything picked up by a numpty in a supermarket will lack a barcode. Sales assistants will then have to be despatched to far corners of the shop to check the prices of the obscure products chosen by the numpty.

Paying by cheque etc.

Numpties like to hold up the queue snaking round the supermarket behind them for as long as possible by opting to pay by a series of time-consuming methods. These include paying by cheque, paying using a small sack full of loose change, paying using currency which the till assistant has never seen before in their life but which the numpty assures them is legal tender, or paying using several hundred special offer coupons, each of which has to be slowly read and checked.

The forgotten wallet or purse

After doing enough shopping for the next year and putting it all through the checkout, the numpty will pat their pockets before realizing they have left their wallet or purse at home.

Forgetting to pick up their change

Numpties are among the world's greatest tippers. This is not, however, done in a spirit of generosity. Instead, it is done in a spirit of sudden forgetfulness. This is then followed a few minutes later by a spirit of extreme crossness when they realize they failed to pick up £17.68 in change at the supermarket. Numpties are therefore for ever rushing back into shops they have recently left to try and reclaim their change before it's too late. Alternatively they are for ever being chased out of shops by cashiers and well-meaning fellow-shoppers attempting to give them back the change which they have just left behind. The numpties will, however, misinterpret this and presume that they are being chased by a store detective attempting to apprehend them for some misdeed. The numpties will thus run away as quickly as they can from the kind person trying to return their change, who will quickly become exhausted by the effort of running while carrying a large weight of clanking coins.

Knocking over a display

If there is a pile of baked bean tins carefully balanced on top of one another in a six-foot-high stack in the middle of the supermarket, a numpty will be irresistibly drawn to the tin right in the middle. Even though the tins are all identical, the numpty will mysteriously be aware that the can right in the centre of this leguminous mountain contains the most perfect and flavoursome beans. And so the oversize game of Jenga commences.

Numpties do not even require specially constructed displays to cause mayhem. Any item that a numpty picks off the shelf will prove to be a keystone that was holding everything else around it in place. Once this single item is removed from the shelf, there is a slow rumbling of the neighbouring tins, bottles and packets. One by one they begin to cascade into the empty space the numpty has opened until an avalanche of produce comes tumbling into the aisles, causing everyone in the vicinity to run for cover.

Don't say 'Numpty', say...

- A few beans short of a casserole.

- A few sandwiches short of a picnic.

- A few beers short of a six-pack.

- A sausage short of a barbecue.

- A teabag short of a pot.

- A handle short of a suitcase.

- A few French fries short of a Happy Meal.

- A few bricks short of a load.

- Two bob short of a pound.

- Two playing cards short of a deck.

- Two rungs short of a ladder.

- Two clowns short of a circus.

- Three chickens short of a henhouse.

- A few Smarties short of a tube.

5

The Wonderful World of Numpty

Numpty celebrities

Constantly bumping into things as a result of wearing sunglasses even when they are indoors at night time.

Almost drowning as a result of trying to snort "Coke."

Finding themselves stuck permanently in a crouching position after trying to leave their handprint on the Hollywood Walk Of Fame and the cement drying too quickly.

Discovering that the multi-million pound house they thought they had bought in Beverley Hills is in fact in Beverly, East Yorkshire.

Having cosmetic surgery to give themselves a new nose but then discovering their surgeon didn't remove the old one in the process (thus leaving them with two noses and four nostrils).

Getting themselves a part in the latest Blockbuster movie and then discovering that it is in fact an advert for a video rental shop.

Being told their face will be on the front of all the glossies and then discovering that this is because they are going to be the new face of Dulux paint.

Difficulties Encountered by A Numpty Criminal

Trying to hold up a bank with a sawn-off shotgun but then discovering he had sawn off the wrong end.

Trying to hold up a bank with a stocking over his head but then discovering the stocking had too high a denier rating so he couldn't see anything.

Trying to hold up a bank with an accomplice using a pair of tights stretched over each of their heads at the same time.

Holding up a bank and presenting his demands on a piece of headed paper pre-printed with his full name and address.

Telling no-one in the bank to move or he'll shoot and then shooting his accomplice when he moved.

Attempting to shoot through a lock only for the bullet to ricochet straight back into his stomach.

Standing in an identity parade and then calling out 'Yes, that's the woman I robbed' when the victim entered the room.

Finally making a deathbed confession for all the crimes he got away with only to then make a full recovery.

So where did all these Numpties come from?

Scientists believe that *homo numptimus* is the ancient species of slightly dim humans who are the ancestors of all numpties living in the world today.

They are also known as homo not-so-sapiens, *homo thick-as-two-short-planks-iens* or 'the lot who made Neanderthals look brainy and good-looking'.

Superficially, *homo numptimus* would have looked similar to modern man, but with a slightly more gormless and apologetic expression all over his hairy caveman face.

Homo numptimus skulls that have been excavated are of similar dimensions to those of modern man but with the difference that they are completely solid. The *homo numptimus* skull thus provides so much protection for the brain that no room was left to fit the brain in. This complete absence of a brain cavity is believed to have evolved in response to ancient numpties continually bumping their heads on the roof of their caves.

Homo numptimus is believed to have split off from the main branch of *homo sapiens* about 80,000 years ago. The main branch of *homo sapiens* didn't argue. Archaeologists are divided on the reason for the split. Some believe it may have been because *homo sapiens* had decided they didn't want to be associated with this bunch of idiots any more. Others say that the split occurred because *homo numptimus* got a bit lost while trying to find his way back home to the cave one night and thus had to settle down and start a new species from scratch in a new location.

Homo numptimus is nevertheless believed to have been present at the precise moment in history when human beings made many significant advances, such as discovering the secret of fire. Unfortunately, a moment after this *homo numptimus* spilled the contents of a cask of water over the flames, thereby extinguishing the fire and putting human development back 50,000 years.

Evidence also exists that *homo numptimus* was present at the exact location where the wheel was first invented. A complete *homo numptimus* skeleton has indeed been found buried nearby with a tyre track running straight over the top of it.

Further evidence of the existence of homo numptimus is found in ancient cave paintings. In the famous painting of aurochs on a cave wall in Lascaux, France, dated to 15,000 to 10,000 BC, *homo numptimus* can clearly be seen lying face-down beneath the animals as they trample over him. In the cave paintings of bulls found at Altamira in Spain, a numpty is depicted trying to milk one of the animals. Among the images of human hands printed on the walls at Pech Merle cave in France is the image of a *homo numptimus* hand. Alone among ancient cave hand prints, the *homo numptimus* hand is the only one covered in burns and sores as a result of having been stuck in the fire immediately beforehand to get it sooty enough to leave a really good print.

Ancient numpties are also believed to have left imprints of their faces on cave walls although this was as a result of continually bashing their faces into the rock because they weren't looking where they were going.

Periods in the ancient history of homo numptimus	
The Stone Age	Period when most homo numptimus skeletons to have been excavated show evidence of having been killed by stones dropping on their heads.
The Iron Age	Period when most homo numptimus skeletons to have been excavated show evidence of their clothes having scorch marks all over them.
The Bronze Age	Period when most homo numptimus skeletons to have been excavated show evidence of having died through over exposure to tanning.
The Palaeolithic Era	Period when most homo numptimus skeletons to have been excavated show evidence of having died after tripping over buckets (or pails).
The Ice Age	Period when most homo numptimus skeletons to have been excavated show evidence of having died as a result of slipping over.
The Neolithic Era	Period when most homo numptimus skeletons to have been excavated show evidence of having died as a result of knee injuries (which the numpties were unable to spell properly).

Notable Numpties in history

Romulus Numptius

Ancient Roman impresario who in the second century BC arranged a visit by what he thought was a popular touring circus act called Hannibal and His Elephants.

Pliny the Numpty

Ancient Roman soothsayer who advised Julius Caesar that the Ides of March would be the perfect day to go down to the senate, and not to take any guards because Brutus could be trusted to look after him.

Maximus Numptimus

Chief planning officer for Pompeii New Town.

Alfred the Numpty

Head of tourism for the north east of England in the late 8th century who headed a campaign to encourage Vikings to visit the area for their holidays.

Godwin Numptyson

King Harold's bodyguard and stunt double at the Battle of Hastings who reportedly remarked to the king, 'Oo! Look at that arrow heading straight towards you!', closely followed by 'Don't worry; they couldn't hit a thing from that distance.'

Ricardo di Numptini

Owner in the late 14th century of a Sicilian pet shop called Black Rats'R'Us specializing in the import of black rats from the Far East, just before the outbreak of the bubonic plague.

Philip of Numptania

World's oldest man during the 14th century and official peace negotiator for the duration of the 100 Years' War.

Edmund of Numpty

Got the wrong end of the stick during the War of the Roses and spent 30 years travelling round England attacking florists.

Thomas Numptyman

Official marriage guidance counsellor at the court of King Henry VIII.

Francis Numptyman

Brother of Thomas. Henry VIII's personal trainer, dietician and anger management counsellor.

Michelnumptelo

As a result of a mix-up over a decorating contract for the pope's toilet, he painted the ceiling of the Sistine Chapel with mildew-resistant whitewash shortly after Michelangelo had finished work on it.

Sir Walter Numpteigh

Attempted unsuccessfully to popularize smoking potatoes. Beheaded himself by accident one day while putting on an over-tight, too heavily starched ruff.

Guido Numpts

Forgotten conspirator involved in the Gunpowder Plot. Asked the completely innocent Guy Fawkes to watch some barrels for him in the basement of the Houses of Parliament while he nipped home to get a firelighter.

Angus McNumpty

A painter and shortbread manufacturer who repeatedly held up the Jacobite army's advance towards London by insisting that Bonnie Prince Charlie pose for a series of illustrations that could be used on promotional tins of shortbread.

Samuel Numptys

Fire prevention officer at the time of the Great Fire of London with special responsibility for the maintenance of hydrants in the Pudding Lane area.

Dr Joseph Numptierre

Inventor of the guillotine. Accidentally started the French Revolution when he got his friend King Louis XVI to pose for a publicity stunt with his head sticking through his new invention, only for disaster to strike.

Captain Numpty

Famously told Admiral Nelson during the Battle of Trafalgar, 'Don't worry, sir. They couldn't hit a thing from that distance.' Believed to be a direct descendant of Godwin Numptyson.

Eric Numptyfellow

Outdoor enthusiast who was camping in the Waterloo area of Belgium in June 1815 and got involved in a major battle when he went over to complain about the noise that was going on in the next field.

Napoleon Numptyparte

Was exiled on the Island of St Helena for six years after getting blown out to sea on a pedalo he had hired while on holiday at Eastbourne.

George Numptyson

Inventor of steam-driven trousers. Also the first man to travel over 30mph vertically while wearing steam-driven trousers and the first man to die as a result of wearing steam-driven trousers.

Gustavus von Numpty

Early 20th-century German psychologist who specialized in helping improve the self-confidence of his patients, such as the young, mild-mannered Adolf Hitler.

Did you hear about the Numpty...

- ...who took up meditation because he said it was better than sitting around all day doing nothing?

- ...who was found with 87 bumps on his head after trying to hang himself using an elastic rope?

- ...who saw a sign outside a police station saying 'Man Wanted For Robbery', so he went in and applied for the job?

- ...who became the world's most unsuccessful forger after filing the corners off hundreds of 50p pieces to turn them into 10p pieces?

- ...who applied for a job as a bin man because he thought they only worked one morning a week?

- ...who turned down the chance of a round-the-world cruise because he said he had no way of getting back?

- ...who won a gold medal at the Olympics and was so proud he had it bronzed?

- ...who locked his keys in his car, so it took him eight hours to get his family out?

6

Numpty about
the house

Numpty about the house

So after you arrive home from a hard day working or shopping among numpties, can you at last close your front door, shut the numpties out and relax in your own private numpty-free zone? No, of course you can't. The numpties will already be in your home waiting for you.

Maybe you have a numpty lodger, perhaps a numpty mum and dad; it could even be that your partner is a numpty and together you plan to unleash a brood of little numpties on the world.

Either way, you have a numpty in your house. You have someone in the building who will leave roller skates and other little booby-traps lying around the place for you to slip over or bump into. You have someone who produces an extraordinary amount of mess but who never thinks of clearing up. You have someone who is capable of breaking anything in the house just by looking at it. Basically, you have someone in your house who is clearly capable of destroying it from within.

Your in-house numpty may then go on to install semi-permanent works of numptiness in your home such as painting the living room a shade of violent puce or nailing up a set of handy shelves across the front of your television.

So it seems that you have allowed one or more numpties to share your home. You probably even made the mistake of giving them a key to your front door. They probably went on to lose this on one or more occasions and you had to replace it for them...

Why have you chosen to shelter a numpty?

Is it an act of charity that you are performing on behalf of the numpty in question whom you have taken in like a sad-looking puppy from the dog shelter, or are you doing it as an act of self-sacrifice to shield the rest of society from the numpty that lurks behind your door? More to the point, what sort of domestic numpty behaviour will you therefore have to endure on a daily basis?

Leaving a roller skate on the stairs

Numpties believe the stairs are the ideal storage place for roller skates and so, while walking downstairs in a hurry, you will often discover that a numpty has left a skate waiting for you. You will become aware of this midway through your descent of the stairs when you notice that you have unwittingly donned wheeled footwear and the speed at which you are travelling has suddenly accelerated to 90 mph.

White circles on the dining table

Numpties will never remember to use a drinks mat when they put their sopping wet glasses and cups down on your most expensive polished wooden surfaces.

Leaning backwards on chairs

Numpties defy convention and will refuse to sit in a four-legged chair in the normal manner. Instead they will lean back in the chair, attempting to balance precariously on two legs for as long as possible before the sound of splintering wood comes from beneath them or they simply tip over backwards into the fireplace.

Rearranging the furniture

Numpties like to do this while you are out of the room. Go out for five minutes to make a cup of tea and when you return you will find that a numpty has decided to completely redesign your living room. Left alone for a moment it will occur to a numpty that the sofa would look nicer at a different angle, the TV should face the other way and the coffee table would be ideally placed in the middle of the doorway.

You will be able to admire all these changes to the décor as you trip over the top of them, go flying and land with a smack where the rug used to be.

Leaving an upturned electric plug on the floor

There is nothing more painful than stepping in bare feet on to the upturned prongs of an electric plug. Those who share their houses with numpties will experience this sensation regularly and will end up with the imprint of three pins permanently etched on the base of their feet.

Leaving electrical appliances switched on

Numpties are unaware that electrical appliances have Off switches. Your in-house numpty will therefore leave lights, televisions, computers, cookers, hair dryers and anything else they can find running for many hours after they switched them on and then decided to go and do something else instead. The amount of power you are getting through would be terrifying, but luckily the dials on your electric meter will be spinning too fast for you to read them.

Those who live with numpties will therefore have to make regular patrols switching electrical items off. When going on holiday, however, your personal numpty will be sure to leave some appliance switched on to maximum, and thus when you return from three weeks in the sun you will find a three-bar electric fire has been left on for the entire time you have been away. Ironically, it will now be even hotter in your home than it was on holiday and the electricity used will cost more than your trip abroad.

Placing a rug on a polished floor

Numpties like to keep us moving about the house as quickly as possible by leaving roller skates on the stairs or by setting fire to the kitchen. Another method numpties think will help us move from room to room more speedily is to leave a rug on a nice polished wooden floor. Walk a bit too quickly through the hallway of any house where a numpty lives and you'll find yourself unexpectedly lying flat on your front doing an indoor toboggan run towards the back door.

Leaving a drink on the floor

Numpties like to leave half-finished cups of tea and other drinks on the floor rather than placing them on a table or washing them and putting them away in a cupboard. Anyone who passes within a few yards of the cup will then somehow catch the drink with their toe and send it flying across the room. Even just half a cup will turn out to be capable of recolouring an unusually large area of carpet.

Hoarding old rubbish

Numpties will hoard mounds of old rubbish in your home for no obvious reason. Your house will thus become a museum of discarded mobile phones, broken electrical appliances and old copies of the Radio Times. When asked, numpties will claim these items must be kept as they definitely intend to use them again and/or one day they will be immensely valuable.

Putting your stuff out in the bin

When it comes to *your* most precious possessions, however, your numpty housemate will seem keen to get rid of them as quickly as possible. They will therefore regularly break, lose or accidentally put out for the recycling any items that you particularly hold dear.

Setting off the burglar alarm

Your house numpty will set off your burglar alarm several times a day as a result of accidents, assorted acts of idiocy and simply walking through the front door. They will, however, never be able to switch the alarm off, as they will be incapable of memorizing the four-digit code required to do so.

Offering a warm welcome to unwelcome callers

Nobody wants strange people knocking on their door trying to sell them things, switch their energy supplier or encouraging them to join their coven. Most people don't even want people that they know knocking on their door. Your in-house numpty will be happily unaware that you should close the door on these callers as soon as you hear the words, 'How are you today?' Instead, your numpty about the house will give these intruders the cheeriest welcome they've had all day. He'll take a pity on any greasy salesmen, rough-looking individuals selling dusters or pairs of old crones clutching religious pamphlets who come knocking. Before they know it, these people will have been invited into your living room and given a nice cup of tea and a biscuit. Then, when you get home, your friendly in-house numpty will inform you that there is somebody waiting to see you who wants to talk to you... possibly for a very long time.

Thanks again, numpties!

Ways in which Numpties will leave the house to make life slightly easier for burglars

- All the doors and windows left open.

- All the doors and windows locked but with a large Post-It note stuck on the front door saying where the key is hidden.

- The door locked with the key hidden on a string just inside the letterbox.

- The door locked with the key hidden on a string just outside the letterbox.

- All the doors and windows left locked but the garden shed fully accessible with its range of ladders, tools and other handy housebreaking equipment.

- The burglar alarm left switched off.

- The burglar alarm left switched on but with the instruction book and the code to disable it left next to it.

- A status update left on Facebook saying they are leaving the house, giving the precise length of time they will be out and detailing the full postal address of the property.

Numpty checklist: getting up in the morning

- A numpty should never set his alarm clock properly, thereby ensuring a minimum amount of time to get ready in the morning.

- The numpty's alarm should nevertheless be positioned on the bedside table so close to his ear that it will give him a heart attack when it goes off.

- Numpties should never bother pulling the curtains across their bedroom window, to ensure they expose themselves to the neighbours immediately they climb out of bed.

- Numpties should possess heavily worn pairs of slippers to make tripping down the stairs almost inevitable.

- Numpties should have a plentiful supply of past-its-sell-by-date milk in their fridges ready to pour over their Corn Flakes.

- Numpties should never check the temperature of the shower before jumping in, thereby providing an exciting surprise when it turns out to be scalding hot or icy cold.

- Numpties should make sure there is not a single sheet of toilet paper left in the house ready for the morning.

Telltale signs that a Numpty has been using your household appliances

Television

Will not work because the remote control has been lost, never to be found again. If you do manage to switch it on you will find that all pre-set channels have been retuned and a security system has been initialized, requiring you to put in a password before you can watch anything (the numpty responsible will, of course, have forgotten the password chosen).

Telephone

Will not work because it was not replaced in its charger when the numpty finished his/her last call. The numpty may also have failed to hang up their last call, which will have been to the speaking clock in Australia.

Radio

Will come on at a level of volume so deafening you will be left temporarily stunned.

Computer

Will take six hours to come on and then do nothing but link to a Russian porn site while telling you, you have to pay $1,000 to have a new anti-virus system installed.

Great moments in Numpty history

The telephone

1st July 1875	Alexander Graham Bell invents the world's first telephone.
2nd July 1875	A numpty dials the world's first wrong number.
3rd July 1875	A numpty invents telesales. Alexander Graham Bell, the owner of the world's only telephone, is plagued by telephone calls for double glazing and strange men asking if he is interested in consolidating his debts into one single easy monthly payment.
4th July 1875	Alexander Graham Bell gets so fed up he has to have his phone disconnected.
7th January 1927	First transatlantic telephone call is made.
8th January 1927	First transatlantic telephone call is made by a numpty using someone else's phone while they were away from their desk.
17th June 1946	The first mobile phone call is made.
18th June 1946	A numpty invents the world's first really irritating mobile phone ringtone.

Domestic Science skills for Numpties

Cookery

There are two basic styles of numpty cookery.

Firstly, there is the classic numpty cooking method of burning the entire meal into a smouldering pile of charcoal. The other basic numpty recipe is to serve food in a completely uncooked state. Numpty food is therefore predominantly crunchy in texture, either because it has the consistency of anthracite or because it still contains shards of ice.

Very occasionally numpties will manage to cook a meal that is perfect in every way. Unfortunately they will then immediately drop this on the filthy kitchen floor while taking it out of the oven, either through sheer clumsiness or because they forgot that their oven mitts had a massive hole in them.

Numpties, however, never abandon hope and will still attempt to serve the meal. They will do this even if they have to scoop the food back up with a dustpan and brush or fight to pull it back out of the dog's mouth before dishing it out to their astonished guests.

Laundry

Washing machines were invented to help you avoid having to buy new clothes every time your old ones got a bit smelly. Numpties, however, manage to sidestep this advantage.

They are the masters of secretly slipping a bright red item into every whites wash. Beneficiaries of the numpty wash are walking around right now wearing shirts and underwear that should be white but are instead slightly embarrassed-looking.

And if your branch of Numpty-sons The Cleaners fail to turn your grundies salmon-coloured, don't worry. Their other great trick is to boil-wash any of your delicate items. You will then find a selection of what appear to be doll's clothes hanging up in your wardrobe. You will wonder for a moment if your body has expanded by some extraordinary amount over the past couple of days.

And if none of these ploys work there's always the numpty's final trick: turn the steam iron up to maximum so you find you clothes all have a distinctive black iron-shaped motif singed through them.

Cleaning

Numpties can find a myriad improper uses for vacuum cleaners including vacuuming hard surfaces, up walls and outside in the garden.

Sucking up puddles of water from the floor is another favourite, which can quickly lead either to electrocution or having to buy a new vacuum cleaner.

Numpties can cause more destruction by attempting to use the vacuum cleaner's attachments on delicate ornaments, the family pet or their own bodies.

Numpties also like to use the vacuum attachments on objects that are small enough to be sucked into the vacuum cleaner (again including certain parts of their own bodies and certain family pets).

You will know if a numpty has been using your vacuum cleaner because when it is switched on again it will make various strange noises. These include rattling, rasping and squeaking (possibly from the small pet lost somewhere inside).

After a numpty has finished vacuuming, happy hours can then be spent going by hand through the dust and dirt emptied from the cleaner while searching for lost precious items (or pets).

Storage

Numpties never properly replace lids on jars or bottles when they put them back in the cupboard, and so the next time they are taken out they go flying, bouncing and crashing across the kitchen floor.

Numpties also like to open breakfast cereal packets at both ends so their contents empty across the floor while en route from the cupboard to your bowl.

Numpties never clear out their cupboards and are frequently delighted to rediscover no longer available brands of foodstuffs, often pre-dating the introduction of use-by dates, which they then excitedly serve to any visiting guests.

Cupboards can also be booby-trapped by numpties with their contents left leaning against the doors ready to tumble out as soon as they are opened.

Another booby-trap method used by numpties is to surreptitiously open a cupboard door while someone is bending over to get something from a shelf or cupboard below. Then when this individual stands up again they will crack their head against the edge of the door left open above them.

Cold storage

Numpties will leave cartons of liquid on their sides in the fridge so they slowly empty their contents over whatever lies beneath.

Anything stored on a lower shelf of your fridge will therefore be discovered marinating in a puddle of milk and orange juice.

Numpties will also perform a similar and even more dangerous trick, with lumps of raw meat left on the top shelf of the fridge to drip and flavour all that lies below.

The numpty's icebox is never defrosted, with the result that it now contains two massive glaciers between which only wafer-thin items can be fitted.

Numpties will never remember to check the use-by date on any items stored in their fridge. Thus goods dating back to the last century will gradually be pushed to the back or bottom of the fridge. There they will wither and moulder until they turn into puddles of gloop or evolve into life forms capable of walking out of the fridge on their own.

Washing-up

Numpties like washing-up, as they see it as a sort of bubble bath for dirty dishes.

Dishes, however, do not like being washed up by numpties because they are extremely unlikely to survive the process.

The numpty method of washing up is to fill the sink to overflowing with water plus enough washing-up liquid to produce a three-foot-high mound of bubbles before bashing the crockery and glasses against the taps and each other until the dirt drops off them or they shatter (whichever comes first).

Numpties are frequently overwhelmed by the fruity fragrances of washing-up liquids. A numpty will find the aromas of lemon, apple or tangerine irresistible and glug down half a cupful of the delicious mixture. Numpties will often make this mistake on more than one occasion.

If you have to finish off the washing-up for a numpty, don't forget they will have left a sharp object such as a tin lid at the bottom of the bowl ready to slice your fingers off.

Kitchen equipment

Blenders

Numpties never feel any need to put the lid on a blender before switching it on. The material for blending will then be served straight from the blender and can easily be licked off walls, ceilings, floors and passers-by.

Knives

These will never be lost in a numpty household because there will always be a trail of blood leading to them.

Dishwasher

Do not ask a numpty to load your dishwasher for you. Your china tea set will be smashed apart when it goes on to the spin cycle.

Pans

The pans in a numpty household will come with various meals already stuck to them, as the numpty will have burnt several dinners on to their surfaces so intensely they can never be removed.

Toaster

Anyone who uses a toaster that is regularly used by a numpty will discover the dials have inexplicably been set to a level capable of incinerating most metals, let alone bread.

Food mixers

After whisking up a cake mix using an electric mixer, a numpty will be overcome with desire.

He/she will look at the mixer's metal beaters, dripping with delicious unbaked cake mix, and will be unable to resist having a lick. This is another very bad numpty idea. Often they will do this while the beaters are still slowing to a halt. Their tongue will then become caught and wrapped in and out of the prongs.

Sometimes a numpty will be more careful and wait until the beaters have stopped moving before sticking their tongue through them. In such cases, however, the numpty will then accidentally switch the mixer back on again, ensuring that their tongue is drawn out, wrapped round the metal prongs and tied in a knot.

For this reason numpties who enjoy baking will invariably possess tongues several times longer than the human average.

This is all bad enough with an electrical device, but certain numpties are known to have endured this self-inflicted injury while using hand-held mixers.

The Numpty guide to cleaning

Bleach

Use indiscriminately on all surfaces, particularly those for which the bottle specifically says it should not be used. Apply by hand without the use of rubber gloves. Use neat and leave to dry on lavatory seats, but always remember not to warn others you have done this.

Soapy water

Use in copious amounts to clean electrical appliances, preferably while they are switched on and someone is using them.

Dish cloth

Can be used to wash dishes, wipe kitchen surfaces, clean shoes and mop up cat sick without ever needing to be cleaned or replaced.

Metal scourers

Use metal scourers on the surfaces of non-stick pans and to get stubborn spots of gravy off the polished wooden dining table. With a little bit of perseverance and elbow-grease they can also be used to remove tattoos.

Lemon-scented cream cleaner

The popular cream cleaner Jif had to be renamed Cif because numpties kept squirting it over their pancakes on Shrove Tuesday.

More Numpty culinary disasters

- Trying to pour the contents of a burning chip pan down the sink.

- Leaving forgotten leftovers in the oven for several weeks until they can only be removed by men dressed in biological protection suits.

- Heating up food in the microwave without any cover, so it indicates when it is ready by splattering over the inside of the door.

- Leaving the electric cooker rings still switched on a low heat and then leaning or sitting on them.

- Forgetting about anything left simmering on the hob until it sets off the smoke alarms in not only your own but your neighbour's house as well.

- Never wiping the hob clean, so eventually it becomes possible to fry things on the cooker without the use of any additional oil... or pan.

- Warming plates on the hob until they are ready to melt your fingers when you pick them up.

- Fiddling with the timer on the cooker so the oven switches itself off or on at totally unexpected moments.

Ways in which a Numpty may block your toilet

- With every sheet of toilet roll you had in the house.

- With their mobile phone, which they had accidentally dropped in the bowl.

- With their own fist, while trying to retrieve their mobile phone from round the S-bend.

- With the snapped-off head of your toilet brush, broken while attempting to shift an earlier blockage.

- With the contents of the bowl of pot-pourri you had balanced on the cistern and which they had accidentally tipped into the toilet.

- With their foot, while attempting to climb up to open a window.

- With their bottom, as a result of not making sure the seat was down before they sat on it.

- With several pounds of mashed-up Dundee cake, while conducting an experiment to test the power of your flush.

- With their head, during a misguided attempt to rinse shampoo from their hair after the shower stopped working.

The Numpty guide to DIY

Numpties usually have to do it themselves. This is because everyone else knows how dangerous it is to stand anywhere near them while they are using a drill, hammer or even a drawing pin.

It is therefore extremely difficult for numpties to get anyone to come and help them: at least, that is, until the inevitable moment when the emergency services have to be called.

Shelves

Numpties always like to put up shelves at a very slight angle. This should be almost imperceptible at first, but it will soon become annoyingly apparent, as any round objects placed on the shelf will roll towards to one end before crashing to their doom.

Numpties choose the material they use for shelving very carefully in order to make sure they are completely inadequate to bear the loads that are placed on them. Numpty-fitted shelves will therefore crash to the ground in the middle of the night or, alternatively, just as an elderly member of the family is passing by beneath them.

Screws

When driving in screws, numpties make sure they force the head of the screw so hard that it ends up completely obliterated. This then makes it extremely difficult to remove the screw at any point in the future.

Another good way to achieve this end is to put the screw in using a hammer rather than a screwdriver.

Rawlplugs are used to secure screws in walls, but not by numpties. Numpties prefer to stick screws straight into the wall. This provides the added advantage that the screw can henceforth be slid in and out of the hole without any need for a screwdriver.

Paint

There are an extraordinary range of different paints currently on the market. This makes it easy for numpties to find exactly the wrong sort of paint to use on any particular job. Numpties will thus find a variety of paint that seemingly never dries, before applying this liberally to all surfaces including carpets, furniture, clothes, hands, faces and pets.

Drills

Before drilling a hole, a numpty will very carefully test a wall's thickness and substance. Once he has done this the numpty will suddenly thrust his drill bit right through the wall into the next room. If the drill can be made to pass through a water pipe or electricity cable on the way, then so much the better.

In the unlikely event that a numpty manages to successfully drill a hole through a wall or piece of wood, the numpty will become overwhelmed by the desire to stick his finger through it. The numpty finger will slip easily into the hole in one direction but then become stuck fast. The numpty will then attempt to drill clumsily around the first hole in a terrifying attempt to increase the size of the hole. The numpty may eventually manage to retrieve his finger by this method, although the finger may then have to be reassembled by a skilled team of surgeons.

Alternatively, a dismembered numpty's finger will be left sticking out of your wall forever.

Woodwork

Numpties cannot run their hands over a piece of wood without somehow immediately filling their fingers with several hundred splinters. Some numpties only have to walk in the vicinity of a piece of wood in order to splinter themselves. It is as though the splinters are somehow drawn towards the numpty body by some sort of wood-based magnetism, possibly emanating from the large lump of wood that forms the brain of the numpty.

Hammers

The numpty method of hammering is, of course, to place a thumb firmly over the head of a nail a moment before attempting to whack it into place. This method has two advantages. The nail is held firmly in place by the thumb that is holding it. Secondly, the thumb will serve as a target for the hammering. This will become increasingly easy; the thumb will rapidly grow in size and deepen in colour, thus making it much easier to aim at.

Numpties will also, of course, manage to nail themselves to whatever surface they are working on.

7

Numpty
on holiday

How to spot a Numpty on holiday

Airport alert

After sitting round for hours waiting to check in for their long-awaited holiday abroad, numpties will be unable to resist making a hilarious joke about a bomb being hidden in their luggage. Cue another few hours' delay, this time in the presence of some angry-looking officials.

Sunburn

After just a short period of time in a hot climate, the sun will help numpties stand out in a crowd by making them turn a bright red. Any parts of the numpty body not on show will, however, remain their usual milk-white colour, making the numpty appear to be wearing a white T-shirt and pants even when they are completely naked.

Holiday tack

Numpties will also distinguish themselves while on holiday by buying and wearing the tackiest items of clothing available locally, including 'Kiss Me Kwik' hats and the most vomit-inducing Hawaiian shirts. It is almost as though these items were designed specifically with the numpty tourist in mind.

Volume

Another good way to spot numpty holidaymakers is by the amount of noise they produce. Numpties are often determined to enjoy their holiday as loudly as possible.

Immersion in the local culture

Ten minutes after arrival in a foreign location, numpty holidaymakers may start speaking in a bad imitation of the local accent. They may then go on to adopt local customs, style of dress, dietary restrictions, religious observances, superstitions and sign up to join the national army even though they are only visiting the country for a three-night mini-break.

Non-immersion in the local culture

Alternatively, the numpty holidaymaker may spend their entire visit seeking out shops, cafés and bars providing exclusively British cuisine. The numpty will thus have travelled thousands of miles to an exotic foreign location to spend their holiday in a chip shop.

Tummy trouble

The other place a numpty will spend their holiday is sitting on the toilet, as a result of ill-advised dietary choices on their first day.

Things a Numpty is likely to forget on holiday

- The date and time of their flight.

- Their passport, tickets, money etc.

- The key to their hotel room door every time they go down to breakfast.

- What time the hotel finishes serving breakfast.

- Their sun cream and the length of time it is advisable to be out in the sun.

- The way back to their hotel every time they go out.

- The name of their hotel so they can ask for directions back.

- The fact that they cannot swim.

- How much alcohol they can consume without making themselves horribly sick.

- Where they parked their car when they left it at the airport.

- Which side of the road we drive on in this country.

Ways Numpties will attempt to make themselves understood to foreigners

- By talking very loudly.

- By talking very slowly.

- By speaking in English but adopting a very bad foreign accent.

- By talking like a character from an old Tarzan film.

- By miming and indicating objects some of which are not within view, and possibly several miles away.

- By doing a slow, extended and extremely bizarre mime performance.

- By getting so confused during their mime performance that they start thinking they're on the TV show Give Us A Clue.

- By talking fluently in a foreign language (but sadly not the foreign language spoken by the person they are talking to).

- By repeating themselves endlessly as though the foreign person will eventually start to understand them.

8

Is your partner a Numpty?

How to tell if your partner is a Numpty

It is usually not difficult to tell if the person with whom you spend your life is a numpty. As soon as you look over at them and see them give you a big, soppy smile back (possibly while dribbling slightly), you will then know the truth in your heart.

And just in case that's not clear enough for you, you will probably hear a voice in your head loudly telling you, 'Oh, my God! I'm shacked up with a numpty!'

- If your love for your partner is tinged with a slight yet continuous sense of pity,

- if you are for ever clearing up after them,

- if you are constantly having to fix things that they have broken,

- if you are constantly tending injuries which they have accidentally inflicted on themselves or on passers-by...

- then it is possible that your partner is a numpty.

Suddenly you will realize your relationship with your partner is not so romantic, but more like caring for a large, non-academically gifted child.

But there is no reason to feel ashamed of love for a numpty. OK, there are certain social occasions when you may have pretended that you weren't with your numpty partner – perhaps one of them was your wedding – but a numpty partner can nevertheless provide many happy moments. These may not seem very happy at the time; indeed, it may be years before you can look back and laugh hysterically at the memory.

Nevertheless, it is good to share your life with a numpty. Numpties need people to look after them, as they are completely unable to fend for themselves. Your relationship may therefore not be distinguished by ongoing erotic passion but, on the plus side, it may be eligible for charitable status.

Of course, your partner may not be a numpty. This could however be even worse. Your partner could be the one looking over at you while thinking, 'Oh, my God! I'm shacked up with a numpty!'

But what are some of the other traits you may notice in a numpty partner?

Forgetting your anniversary

A classic mistake made by numpty partners. You can drop as many hints as you like but your numpty partner will not remember the most special day of the year until the present you bought for them has been smashed or emptied over their numpty head.

Forgetting you exist

A numpty partner may become so comfortable in your presence that they will completely forget you are in the house. This may lead to marital discord. Nothing kills the romance in a relationship more than your numpty partner wandering into the bathroom and taking a dump while you are having a bath. Or vice versa.

Forgetting you're their partner

A numpty partner may forget the true nature of your relationship and treat you instead as their full-time unpaid personal assistant, taxi driver, home handyman, servant or, even worse, their mum or dad.

Forgetting where they live

Numpties may do this as a result of drunken night out with their friends, or simply because they literally forget their way home.

Calling you by a pet name

Without prior consultation, your numpty partner may start calling you by some cringe-making pet name such as Baby Boo, Mrs Squirrel or Captain Love Muffin. This will become particularly excruciating when they start adopting these pseudonyms on birthday, anniversary and Christmas cards which are left on display on the mantelpiece for passing friends, family and workmen to pick up and read.

Your numpty partner will persist in the use of your unwanted pet name over a period of many years. When you are both in your eighties, your numpty partner will still be referring to you as Mushy Poops, although ironically by this stage it may have become more appropriate.

Numpties will persist even if you repeatedly tell them, 'Please don't call me by that name' or 'If you call me that one more time I will commence divorce action.' Eventually divorce papers may indeed have to be drawn up calling for the annulment of the marriage of Colonel Numpty and his wife Mrs Pixie Nose.

Sharing your intimate secrets

If you share any intimate and embarrassing secrets with your numpty partner, your numpty partner will not realize these should be kept private and will pass them on to everyone they meet. You may thus find complete strangers coming up to you in the street and asking if the boil on your left buttock has cleared up yet.

Making a passionate display in a public place

Numpties can be loving partners, but they will often want to display the overwhelming love they feel for you in slightly inappropriate ways, and in even more inappropriate settings. Numpties may therefore become over-amorous with you while waiting at a bus stop, while standing at the checkout in Lidl or while appearing before an industrial tribunal.

Showing off

Another good opportunity for your partner to reveal themselves as a numpty is while doing something dangerously stupid in order to show off to impress you, your friends, any passers-by and any paramedics you will have to call out a few minutes later.

Tattoos

Tattoos may give you a clue that your partner is a numpty. Your partner probably won't have gone so far as to be tattooed with the statement, 'I am a numpty' although you shouldn't put this past them; if, however, you discover that your partner's body is covered in a series of tattoos each showing the name of one of their previous partners, you should beware. Clearly your partner is a numpty.

- Firstly, they have never managed to sustain a relationship and have permanently advertised the fact on their body.

- Secondly, they have repeatedly failed to realize they were unsuited to their current partner.

- Thirdly, despite the fact that their relationship was doomed, they thought it was a good idea to have the name of their partner permanently inscribed on to their skin.

- Fourthly, they have done this more than once. When you look at your numpty partner's body you will realize it resembles a library book with the names of all the people who have previously borrowed it listed on the front page.

Using someone's joke name to their face

You may have an acquaintance to whom you jokingly refer by an amusing name. Your numpty partner will laugh along with you as you regale them with anecdotes about characters to whom you have given nicknames such as Don Corleone, Rumpelstiltskin or Barry Bee Gee. When your numpty partner is introduced to them, however, they will start using this funny name to their face, either out of absentmindedness or because they genuinely believe it is the person's real name.

Telling you what they really think

You ask for an opinion about what you look like, what you're wearing or whether you appear to be putting on weight. Your partner responds with a completely honest answer. What a numpty.

Recalling happy memories of courtship

Particularly when these involved a previous partner.

Dumping you

The numptiest thing your numpty partner can do is to leave you for someone else. The only possible explanation is that they have found someone who is as much of a numpty as they are.

The Numpty lovers' guide

Things that you may find your numpty partner doing at moments of great passion and intimacy:

- Consulting an instruction manual.

- Taking a phone call.

- Taking a video call.

- Pulling a face that you can't help laughing at.

- Suddenly calling out someone else's name very loudly.

- Even worse, suddenly calling out their own name.

- Even even worse, suddenly calling out a pet's name.

- Deciding to perform an impromptu erotic massage using what quickly turns out to be a tube of Deep Heat rub.

- Attempting to perform a physically challenging manoeuvre but then getting stuck and having to be carried out in the same position by paramedics half an hour later.

- Apologizing.

Birthday presents you are likely to receive from a Numpty

- Something you have already got.

- The same thing they gave you last year.

- Something you have no interest in or use for.

- Something you have no interest in or use for, and which you already have because they gave you one of them last year.

- A very large framed photograph of themselves.

- A large tub of something to treat a personal problem you hoped no one else had noticed.

- An item of clothing completely unsuited to your size, style and possibly gender.

- A personalized item inscribed with an incorrect spelling of your own name.

- An item currently stockpiled in huge quantities and being sold off at a massive discount in a local bargain store.

- An item you recently donated to a charity shop.

9

Numpty leaders

Our Numpty leaders

These days, people are no longer surprised by the suggestion that certain politicians are numpties. Instead, they are more likely to be surprised by the suggestion that there are any MPs out there who aren't numpties.

Political life does indeed seem to attract a particular breed of numpty – one with a big head, a thick skin and no sense of shame.

- After all, what sort of person would think they have all the answers to everyone else's problems?

- What sort of person would think they are ideally equipped to tell the rest of us what to do?

- What sort of person would want a job where everything they say and do will be subject to widespread ridicule?

- What sort of person would want to get blamed for everything that goes wrong in the country?

- What sort of person would want a job where millions of us would, given half a chance, pelt them repeatedly with rotten eggs?

Yes, being a numpty must be an essential qualification for candidates applying for political life.

As we have mentioned, the term 'numpty' became popular during Gordon Brown's premiership. Nevertheless, there are numpties of all political persuasions in all parts of the world.

William Hague, George W Bush, Sarah Palin, Silvio Berlusconi and Kim Jong Il of North Korea all have something of the numpty about them, while the thought of Boris Johnson may not bring the words 'Mayor of London' springing to mind quite as readily as 'Numpty of Everywhere'.

Yes, the numpties have taken over the world, and this explains many things. The reason why the planet is in the state it's in is because everywhere you go the Numpty Party is permanently in power. Each day Numpty governments are dreaming up new numpty ideas and putting new numpty policies into law so all of us have to live our lives according to numpty principles. You may indeed wonder which numpties voted for them.

But just what are some of the other ways that our politicians like to demonstrate to the world that they are in fact numpties?

Pretending to like cool bands they've never heard of

No one believed Gordon Brown when he claimed to be a fan of The Arctic Monkeys. Clearly the most modern record that Gordon genuinely owned was a 78rpm disc by Jimmy Shand and his Scottish accordion band.

Dressing in military gear

Numpty MPs cannot resist dressing up in camouflaged outfits whenever they visit a military base. Why is this necessary? If they were visiting a dairy would they feel the need to dress up as a milkman or don a pantomime cow costume?

Baseball caps

Yes, William Hague, we're looking at you. Nothing says 'numpty' better than a baseball cap on top of a bald middle-aged man's head. You might as well get someone to write the word 'numpty' on your shiny scalp with a magic marker.

Punching voters

Who could forget John Prescott punching that idiot with the mullet during the 2001 election? Battering the electorate one by one is surely a very inefficient way of getting them to vote for you.

Failing to answer the question they have just been asked

When asked a tricky question during an interview, a numpty politician will give the answer to a completely different, much easier question that they revised before coming on. They will then get stroppy if anyone points out just how irrelevant their answer was.

Promising one thing, then doing another

Numpty politicians repeatedly promise us nice things when they want us to vote for them and then hit us with not so nice things afterwards. They then expect none of us to mind. They must think we're even thicker than they are.

Not practising what they preach

Only a numpty could fail to realize that if you go round telling people to eat more healthily, it's probably better if your own waistline is under 45 inches. Only a numpty would lecture people on the importance of family values while simultaneously cheating on their wife: and, once again, only a numpty would do any of these things and expect none of the rest of us to notice.

Numpty leaders

Fiddling their expenses

Nothing proves that politicians are numpties better than this. Politicians have chosen to go into a profession in which they know they will be hauled over the coals for the slightest misdemeanour. They have also chosen to go into a profession where every move they make will be subject to intense scrutiny. Having done this, they then think they can get away with everything from petty pilfering to grand larceny. They do this in the belief that either we won't notice, we won't be interested or we won't particularly object to them spending £1,645 of our money on a house for their pet ducks.

Failing to resign

Numpty politicians always think they can keep their jobs no matter how incompetent they have been shown to be. But then they are numpties.

Buggering up the economy and starting wars

At least with most numpties, there is a limit to the amount of damage they can cause.

Getting us to pay for all their numptiness

Which numpty came up with the idea of income tax?

Things That Are Likely To Happen When A Numpty Politician Kisses A Baby During An Election Campaign

The baby will immediately start screaming in abject horror.

The numpty politician will grimace at the wrong moment as though to say 'what an ugly baby'.

The numpty politician will accidentally drop the baby.

The baby will vomit over the numpty politician.

The numpty politician will vomit over the baby.

The numpty politician will drop the baby.

The numpty politician will get confused and kiss the wrong end of the baby.

The numpty politician will realise the baby is in fact his own love-child, the existence of which has to date been kept a closely guarded secret as a result of a super-injunction.

The numpty politician will find himself intellectually outwitted by the baby.

Things A Numpty Politician Will Do Immediately After Being Announced The Winner Of An Election

Demand a recount

Look really fed up and depressed because he doesn't understand that he has won

Pull his shirt up over his face and run round in celebration in front of the other candidates until he falls off the edge of the stage

Drop his pants and wiggle his bare backside at the losing candidates

Make a short victory speech to the assembled voters beginning with the words 'So, ve are zer masterz now!' in a really bad German accent

Make a short victory speech to the assembled voters beginning with the words 'You idiots! What were you thinking voting for me?!' before rolling round on the floor pissing himself laughing for several minutes

Immediately request a list of all the things he can get on parliamentary expenses

Ask who wants to join him for a few drinks to celebrate down at the local brothel

Great moments in Numpty history
Politics

700 BC	Establishment of ancient Greek democracy in Athens.
699 BC	A numpty stands in Athenian by-election on behalf of the Monster Raving Loony Party.
1832	UK Parliamentary reform: Representation of the People Act paves the way for the principle of one man, one vote.
1833	A numpty decides he can't be bothered going out to vote.
1872	The secret ballot paper is introduced in British elections.
1873	The spoilt secret ballot paper is introduced by a numpty (by accident, as a result of trying to make a cross with an unexpectedly messy pencil).
1897	Suffragettes begin chaining themselves to railings to demand votes for women.
1898	A numpty is mistaken for the first male member of the Suffragettes after chaining himself to a railing by accident while trying to lock up his bike.

10

Numpty IQ

If....

- If he blew up a balloon, his head would deflate.

- If he had another brain cell, it'd be lonely.

- If he was any dumber, you'd have to water him.

- If he were any smarter, you could teach him to fetch.

- If stupidity were a crime, he'd be on the Most Wanted list.

- If the government ever declared war on stupidity, he'd get nuked.

- If you gave him a penny for his thoughts, you'd get change.

- If he ever had a bright idea, it would be beginner's luck.

- If you stand close enough to his head, you can hear the ocean.

- If ignorance is bliss, he must be experiencing a near- constant orgasm.

- If he were twice as smart, he'd still be stupid.

The Numpty IQ

- He has an IQ one point above brain death.

- He has an IQ of room temperature.

- Bacteria regularly outscore him on IQ tests.

- He has an IQ lower than his shoe size.

- His IQ is so low, he has to dig for it.

- When his IQ gets up to 50 he should sell.

- He should have a low voice to go with his low IQ.

- He is unable even to spell IQ.

- He thought IQ was the title of the autobiography of the James Bond gadget guy.

- If his brain was removed, his IQ would go up.

- He has an IQ slightly lower than he can count up to.

- He has been forced to resit his IQ test until he at least gets his name right on the front of the paper.

- He thinks IQ is the sound someone makes when they sneeze.

- He thinks the expression IQ is usually followed by the words 'very much'.

- He thinks IQ is the noise made at moments of exertion by martial arts experts.

- He has an IQ so low they had to test for it using depth charges.

- He has an IQ so small they had to use an electron microscope to see it.

- He has an IQ so well hidden a substantial reward has been offered to anyone with information leading to its safe discovery.

- Scientists cannot believe anyone could have an IQ so low and still be able to dribble.

- Scientists cannot believe anyone could have an IQ so low and yet be able to fill in an IQ test answer sheet.

- He would have got a better score in his IQ test if he had left his answer sheet blank.

- His IQ goes up when he is asleep.

Ways in which a Numpty could lose £100

- While attempting to make a cashpoint withdrawal during a hurricane.

- By handing it to a stranger who was just asking the time, but who the numpty assumed was a mugger.

- While holding it above their head and dancing around in excitement at the thought of possessing £100.

- By forgetting they had placed it on the roof of their car while they tried to find their keys.

- While making a cashpoint withdrawal from a machine adjacent to a storm drain.

- While bending over to check a flushing toilet while the £100 was in their breast pocket.

- While standing at the office shredder and daydreaming that they were at the self-service till in the supermarket.

- While attempting to pay a £10 bill while not wearing their glasses.

- While checking if the notes were genuine using a strong magnifying glass on a sunny day.

Did you hear about the Numpty...

- ...who got stranded for an hour on a broken escalator?

- ...who got his arm stuck under a boulder while pot holing, so he tried to free himself by cutting off the other arm?

- ...who got sacked from a banana factory for throwing the bent ones away?

- ...who joined the Sea Scouts and drowned when his tent sank?

- ...who went and looked in the letterbox because his computer told him he had mail?

- ...who put a stamp on a letter he was sending by fax?

- ...who typed a letter on his computer and then covered the screen in Tipp-ex to get rid of the mistakes?

- ...who tried putting in a lightbulb using a hammer?

- ...who collected a load of burnt-out lightbulbs because he was setting up his own darkroom?

- ...who phoned the 8-til-late shop to ask what time they opened.

The Numpty's encyclopaedia of apology

Numpties have many ways of apologizing for their numptiness. Here are a few favourite techniques:

Apologize in advance

In its purest form, the numpty will enter a room and introduce himself to the assembled company thus: 'Hello. I am a numpty. I am very sorry for everything that is about to happen.'

Constant apology

The numpty prefaces everything they do or say with an apology as a very high percentage of their acts and utterances will involve things getting broken, people getting injured and things not being understood.

Numpty immunity

The numpty gives you a cross look as though suggesting that a disaster that they have just perpetrated was in fact your fault, as you knew they were a numpty and should have known the potential consequences of taking them anywhere.

Numpty self-hatred

The numpty falls to their knees sobbing, 'I am such a numpty!' This creates a maudlin moment not unlike that of the Elephant Man suddenly realizing he isn't quite the same as other people.

The confessional apology

After, for example, accidentally setting fire to your house, the numpty tells you, 'I am so sorry. I am such a numpty.' This is not only inadequate in view of the damage caused, but is clearly an attempt by the numpty to play on your sympathy. They are suggesting that their numptiness is a sad affliction, you should pity them, perhaps make a charitable donation towards their care and put the loss of your home down to experience.

The chilling reveal of his true identity

After dropping your 64-piece china tea set or knocking your grandmother into a stream, the numpty turns to you and informs you in a solemn, matter-of-fact manner, 'I'm a numpty.'

The little grimace

Following disaster, the numpty bites his lip or looks pleadingly at you like a mischievous puppy.

The proud boast

Having just caused yet another disastrous accident or conflagration, the numpty loudly proclaims of himself, 'Oh, what a numpty!', A bit like a cricketer calling 'Howzat?' Or a lumberjack shouting 'Timber!'

Numpties of the future

So... what sorts of things will numpties be getting up to in the future?

- Boldly going and buggering things up where no numpty has gone and buggered things up before.

- Absent mindedly leaving both doors of the spaceship airlock open.

- Travelling millions of light years across the universe and then remembering they've left the gas on at home.

- Altering the course of an asteroid that might be on a collision course with Earth to leave it definitely on a collision course with Earth.

- Creating the world's first robot army powerful and intelligent enough to take over the planet.

- Discovering a cure for all known diseases, but then losing the recipe in the recycling bin.

- Contacting alien life-forms from other galaxies, accidentally insulting them and so plunging the Earth into terrible interstellar war.

- Travelling to the edge of the universe and falling off.

Numpties and serial killers

Never make the mistake of hiding from a serial killer with a numpty. If you do, the numpty is likely to do any of the following:

- Ask loudly, 'Has he gone yet?' when the serial killer is still very much within earshot.

- Sneeze at just the wrong moment.

- Respond 'Bless you' if the serial killer sneezes.

- Whisper loudly, 'You wouldn't think he was a serial killer to look at him.'

- Receive a mobile phone call from a numpty friend.

- Give loud, helpful advice such as, 'He's coming! He's just there! Keep absolutely quiet or he'll find us!'

- Tease the serial killer with remarks such as 'Bet you can't find us!' Or 'Peepo, Mr Serial Killer!'

- Start humming a little tune for no reason.

- Fall out of the hiding place.

- Fart and then attempt to blame it on the serial killer.

Don't say 'Numpty', say...

- Not the brightest bulb on the tree.

- Not the brightest crayon in the box.

- Not the brightest penny in the purse.

- Not the brightest star in the sky.

- Not the brightest bulb in the chandelier.

- Not the brightest light in the harbour.

- Not the sharpest knife in the drawer.

- Not the sharpest pencil in the box.

- Not the sharpest pitchfork in the barn.

- Not the sharpest tack in the box.

- Not the quickest ship in the fleet.

- Not the quickest bunny in the forest.

- Not the quickest horse in the stable.

- Not the fastest car in the parking lot.

11

Farewell Numpty

So, farewell, Numpties

And so, dear reader, we have over the preceding pages learnt much about numpties.

We have learnt of their numpty ways, their numpty habits, their numpty traditions and their numpty philosophy of life. And we have learnt how these are all designed to provide the rest of us with irritation, embarrassment and damage to persons and property on an ongoing basis.

If it were not for numpties, non-numpties would live relaxed, trouble-free lives. Non-numpties could sit with their feet up for much of the day. There would be no broken household objects to mend, no mess to clear up, no emergencies at work to sort out, no minor injuries to tend to and no small fires to put out in the boot of your car.

Without numpties, we would have little or nothing to do. Without numpties, armies of repair men and medical professionals would be put out of work.

So, thank you, numpties! Without you, the world economy might be brought to a standstill.

And yet still one grim question remains...

Are You Becoming A Numpty?

You will inevitably meet many numpties during the course of each day. Is it possible, then, that their numptiness could be contagious, and that you are also turning a little bit numpty?

1. When someone calls, 'Oi! You numpty!' Do you:

    a. Look round for the numpty to whom they refer?

    b. Try to ignore them, while worrying that they might mean you?

    c. Turn happily towards them with a big, gormless grin all over your numpty face?

2. When someone tries to explain something to you, do they:

    a. Speak to you in a casual, friendly tone?

    b. Speak to you very slowly?

    c. Use diagrams while continually muttering, 'Give me strength!'?

3. When you visit a shop or someone's home where many delicate, breakable objects are displayed, do the owners:

   a. Welcome you warmly?

   b. Follow you round looking anxious and waiting to catch anything you knock over?

   c. Start filling in the insurance claim form as soon as you walk through the door?

4. When you embrace someone, do they:

   a. Say, 'How lovely to see you.'?

   b. Say, 'Oh. Hello', while looking slightly alarmed?

   c. Say, 'Don't worry; I'll be fine', as they dab blood from the spot where you accidentally just head-butted them?

5. When you offer someone a lift in your car, do they:

   a. Jump straight into the passenger seat?

   b. Make an excuse about how they could do with a walk?

   c. Begin sobbing and saying farewell to their loved ones?

6. Do colleagues at work:

   a. Regularly seek your advice and input?

   b. Seek your advice and input and then do the opposite of anything you suggest?

   c. Regularly lock you in a dark cupboard during meetings and visits from clients?

7. Does your partner:

   a. Treat you as though you are an equal?

   b. Treat you as though you are an ungainly and non-academically gifted overgrown child?

   c. Treat you as though they adopted you from an animal rescue centre?

What happens when Numpties say goodbye and head towards the door

- They go through the door and then a few moments later come back again because they have forgotten their keys.

- They go through the door and then a few moments later come back again because they have just walked into the broom cupboard.

- They find themselves unable to open the door and have to ask for assistance.

- They fiddle with the door for several moments and then turn to reveal the door handle has come off in their hand.

- They fiddle with the door for several moments before someone has to point out to them that the door opens the other way.

- They leave through the door, are gone for several moments and then come back in through a different door, looking confused to find themselves in a room that looks identical to the one they just left.

- They throw the door open, walloping a person who was standing on the other side about to come in.

12

The Numpty Book of Knowledge